THE
POLYAMORY
Workbook

THE
POLYAMORY
Workbook

An Interactive Guide to Setting
BOUNDARIES, Communicating
YOUR NEEDS, and Building Secure, Healthy
OPEN RELATIONSHIPS

Sara Youngblood Gregory

Published by:
Ulysses Press
P.O. Box 3440
Berkeley, CA 94703
www.ulyssespress.com

ISBN: 978-1-64604-406-1
Library of Congress Catalog Number: 2022936244

Printed in the United States by Versa Press
10 9 8 7 6 5 4 3 2 1

Acquisitions editor: Kierra Sondereker
Managing editor: Claire Chun
Project editor: Renee Rutledge
Editor: Kathy Kaiser
Proofreader: Michele Anderson
Front cover design: Ashley Prine
Cover art: © melitas/shutterstock.com
Interior art: Salomé Grasland
Interior design and layout: Winnie Liu

IMPORTANT NOTE TO READERS: This book has been written and published for informational and educational purposes only. It is not intended to serve as medical advice or to be any form of medical treatment. You should always consult with your physician before altering or changing any aspect of your medical treatment. Do not stop or change any prescription medications without the guidance and advice of your physician. Any use of the information in this book is made on the reader's good judgment and is the reader's sole responsibility. This book is not intended to diagnose or treat any medical condition and is not a substitute for a physician. This book is independently authored and published, and no sponsorship or endorsement of this book by, and no affiliation with, any trademarked brands or other products mentioned within is claimed or suggested. All trademarks that appear in this book belong to their respective owners and are used here for informational purposes only. The author and publisher encourage readers to patronize the brands mentioned in this book.

CONTENTS

I believe our imaginations—particularly the parts of our imaginations that hold what we most desire, what brings us pleasure, what makes us scream yes—are where we must seed the future, turn toward justice and liberation, and reprogram ourselves to desire sexually and erotically empowered lives.

—Adrienne Maree Brown

When angels speak of love they tell us it is only by loving that we enter an earthly paradise. They tell us paradise is our home and love our true destiny.

—bell hooks

As a society we are embarrassed by love. We treat it as if it were an obscenity. We reluctantly admit to it. Even saying the word makes us stumble and blush.... Love is the most important thing in our lives, a passion for which we would fight or die, and yet we're reluctant to linger over its names. Without a supple vocabulary, we can't even talk or think about it directly.

—Diane Ackerman

INTRODUCTION

As I sit here now, I'm reminded of the wonderful Jessica Fern, the author of *Polysecure: Attachment, Trauma, and Consensual Nonmonogamy*. Fern says this:

> *"I believe in love. Again and again, I have experienced the power of love to heal, to bridge, to connect and to awaken, as well as the trauma that ensues in its absence. In many ways my life is centered in not just believing in love, but in being love. That is, emanating love as best as I can, moment by moment, interaction by interaction."*

I love talking about love and have made a career writing about it. I began writing in earnest about my love life in 2019, though I had been writing professionally since 2016. I wrote a personal essay for *Vice* called "Chronic Pain Made My Sex Life Better, Not Worse." I thought it might be a difficult piece to write, and I'd never gotten so personal so publicly before. I was coming to terms with a new disability and a new love—both incredible, destabilizing, and transformative forces—in my quiet life. But in one short sitting, the words, scenes, and meaning all came pouring out of me from some dark, warm well. I felt strong. After writing that article, I began taking a more vulnerable and open approach to my work.

Like Fern, I believe in love. I believe the best people love love and love to give love. I believe love should be given freely and received as a gift of respect that is of great value. True love—the kind that doesn't rely on power over someone, fetishization, shoddy intentions, or entitlement—is something I strive to experience and offer every day of my life.

But *knowing* how to love, to offer it up, is harder. The Western world—I'm writing from the United States, where I grew up and received my schooling and socialization—is by and large a sex-negative culture not just distrustful of, but destructive toward, most love that isn't tidy, white, monogamous, cisgender, and heterosexual. But I feel a special, different kind of love when I share my strange, full life with others, either physically or through the page. I share some of myself with you now: how my experiences have shaped this book and what these pages will offer you.

When I was sixteen, and just barely scratching the surface of the queer desire I'd been largely ignoring since childhood, I declared quietly, and only to myself, that I'd never be in a monogamous relationship. I barely had the language to define myself in contrast to monogamy, let alone articulate what I now know about polyamory, relationship anarchy, and relationships based in love and agency. I stuck only with what I could imagine: "not monogamous."

I held on to this knowledge tightly, secretively. I read forums and Reddit threads about being nonmonogamous during my high school years and was, generally, like most other teenagers, messy, lovestruck, and pining. Finally away from an insular high school environment and enrolled in college, I started dating women, bent on exploring my sexuality without rules or regulations. I went to a small, liberal arts college with a high percentage of queer students, where terms such as *ethical nonmonogamy*, *metamour*, and *safer sex* were thrown around like confetti. It was thrilling and absolutely confusing. I started taking gender studies courses, where I learned about women's rights, intersectional feminism, white supremacy, patriarchy, and how these concepts affect the ideas, structures, cultural attitudes, and institutions that surround us all. In and out of the classroom, I began to question everything, from the way I dressed in the morning to why as a little girl I'd dreamed so much about marriage. I connected to myself as a lesbian—in both the political and the personal meanings of the word—and finally began learning about the wider, most colorful strokes of what it means to be a woman.

Feminism, queerness, and polyamory are inseparable for me because they largely arose in my life at the same time. Feminism makes me want to change, challenge, think, and wonder, which reinforces queerness, which makes me want to love and live in new (or more ancient?) ways, which reinforces polyamory by giving me the tools and language for a more communal approach to the love and life I have to offer.

Dating in such an environment was thrilling. Ideas, debates, arguments, parties, and flirtations abounded. But, as with many newbies, my "polyamorous" relationships were mostly a disaster of jealousy, miscommunication, yo-yoing breakups, and (for me) lingering gay trauma. I put the word *polyamorous* in quotes because I now realize I had no idea what I was doing. It was a first attempt at what would ultimately be a very, very long journey, one that continues to this day.

By far, my biggest struggle with ethical nonmonogamy was translating theory into practice. I'd read *The Ethical Slut* and *More Than Two*, both essential reading, but in the early to mid-2010s, conversations about polyamory were just starting to become anywhere near accessible—and what *was* out there didn't necessarily center relationships that were neither cis nor heterosexual. Conversations were also unlikely to deal with the dynamics involved with privilege and power *within* and *outside* these relationships. Now-adays, polyamory coaching, peer support sessions, Instagram and TikTok accounts, zines, books, podcasts, and everything in between are available. The pure amount of information out there now on polyamory is amazing, but it can also be overwhelming. How do you know where you fit in? How do you know what terms and dynamics are right for you? Where do you even start?

Looking back at my college years, I now realize that the crux of my struggles was the *expectations* I had around control and freedom. I expected polyamory to be easy because I'd read a few books. I expected polyamory to be as innate to me as my lesbianism. I expected my partners to be on the same page with me at all times because I expected them to know what *polyamory* meant (as if there were one definition!). I expected to not get jealous because I "didn't believe" in jealousy. I expected to maintain control of my emotions. I expected my partners to maintain control of their emotions. I expected freedom *with* control—both over myself and others. Now I know that this isn't realistic.

In this book, we'll be talking a lot about freedom and control. These two ideas—their push and pull, their connection, and their ultimate impact on our lives—form the basic organizing principle of this book.

Control is inextricably linked to power, nonconsensual domination, and the anxiety of ownership and completeness. Control thinks in black and white, the colors of the absolute. Control looks like self-sabotage, stomachaches from anxiety, and sleepless nights full of what–ifs and *How can I stop that from happening*? Control feels bad because the tighter you hold onto her, the tighter she holds onto you—and the less you're both able to breathe.

The motto of control is "The more I control, the less I get hurt." But decisions based on the desire to control and avoid pain are fear-based, and limit not only your partners' agency but also your own. Control looks like everything we do to prevent pain and jealousy: rule setting, veto power, overbearing policies on sex, guilt-tripping, competition with partners or lovers, and double standards.

Alternatively, the motto of freedom is neither fear based nor power neutral. Freedom acknowledges power dynamics and a larger culture of love scarcity, and chooses instead to prioritize the agency of self and others. Freedom's motto is "Let's be out of control together." In this case, *out of control* does not, of course, mean unethical or dangerous behaviors or relationships, but rather a rejection of the controlling behavior that defines so many relationships, both monogamous and polyamorous. Freedom looks like compersion (defined in the glossary below), negotiation, accountability, and the ability to change and adapt without consequence.

Freedom looks like dealing with the difficult parts of yourself—the jealousy, the pettiness, and the insecurity—and looks toward compassion. Freedom looks like finding positive coping mechanisms, open communication, and a commitment to understand yourself and your loved ones, even as you look toward growth.

Freedom lets go of unrealistic expectations, instead putting that energy toward healthy boundaries with others and the self. Control doubles down on expectations, setting up everyone involved for disappointment.

When I look back on my younger self, I have a lot of compassion. I put myself in a difficult situation. I had unrealistic expectations, limited tools, and no models of queer or lesbian relationships, let alone successful, loving polyamorous relationships. But I also feel gratitude toward that person. She learned, got better, and committed herself to doing the work. The wonderful, loving relationships I now enjoy and endeavor to maintain are due in large part to her. As you read and think on your own relationships—be they monogamous, polyamorous, or something else altogether—I invite you to not look on that past self with judgment. Give yourself patience, compassion, and gratitude.

My partner Salomé always says to me, "I don't care if you make a mistake. I care if you learn from it."

This has become a little mantra of mine. Of course, I *try* not to mess up. But I do. I get impatient. I snap. I forget to communicate something important. I have a bad day and take it out on others. I mope and sometimes whine. But my commitment to not just owning up to my mistakes but making *amends* for them means my partners can trust me. It also means I can trust myself.

Learning from our past actions and mess-ups is an essential part of being in *any* relationship, not just a romantic one. Making mistakes does not mean you can't be polyam or that you're not ready. This book will help you learn about yourself, your triggers, and your insecurities so as to minimize the risk of hurting yourself and others. But you still will, because that's part of the process. It doesn't mean pleasurable, satisfying nonmonogamy can't be for you.

Together, we're going to talk about polyamory. Not just the useful terms and principles of ethical nonmonogamy, but also the ideas that underpin how we *are* in relationships. Our relationship with ourselves. With lovers. With partners. With strangers. With our larger culture and with the world. This book is designed to be interactive, meaning you are involved in the process of creating and engaging with polyamory. I invite you to talk to this book: write in its margins, ask questions back, and argue with what doesn't make sense to you. You'll find open-ended activities, tools, and space for your own thoughts, struggles, and celebrations. Take your time with these activities. Revisit them, share them with partners, and offer them up as conversation starters.

This workbook focuses on the foundational knowledge everyone interested in, or already practicing, polyamory should know: types of nonmonogamy, communication styles, boundary setting, consent, safer sex, metamours and jealousy, pitfalls and red flags, and breakups and lovers. Several chapters begin with a conversation between myself and an expert in polyamory, sex, and much more. Sam of the queer polyam platform *Shrimp*

Teeth talks with me in Chapter 1, author and podcaster Crystal Byrd Farmer converses with me in Chapter 5, and my own polycule members chat with me in Chapter 8.

If you're wondering why this book is so talk heavy, then you're onto something important. Many folks come with the expectation—like I did in my college years—that relationships, sex, love, and trust will fall into place naturally if you have good intentions. Love or sex happens and then, without much work, good communication follows. This couldn't be further from the truth! In reality, 90 percent of polyamory happens in conversation. When I listen actively and with genuine curiosity, hold space, honor my window of tolerance, and approach conflict with an "us versus the problem" mindset, this is when I feel the most deeply satisfied with my life choices and relationships. This space—a mix of reflection, owning up to my bullshit, finding a path to accountability, expressing my needs, and committing myself to respecting and acknowledging my partners—is where my most trusting, secure relationships happen.

It's also important to remember that there is no *one* expert voice on how to make polyamory work for you. Sure, I'm the one writing this book. But I've invited the wisdom of other polyamorous folks so that you'll understand more deeply that polyamory is a personal destination with many, many roads to get there. Not only do personalities differ, but so do our cultural backgrounds, desires, sexualities, races and ethnicities, disability statuses, classes, intentions, and external, structural conditions that we have no control over. My hope is that you will learn from these more community-based conversations and feel more comfortable connecting and working with others to say, *Yes, this is what being polyam means to us.*

Polyamory, like life, isn't something you do alone. In both, you'll need love, resources, and support. This book will give you two—but love is down to you. Now let's get to work.

Let's Take a Moment

Before reading on, take a moment or two to write down your impressions of freedom and control. Use the questions that follow as a guide, and revisit these initial impressions after finishing the workbook.

What is your personal definition of freedom?

What is your personal definition of control?

What does it look like for you to be in a relationship that prioritizes freedom?

What does it look like for you to be in a relationship that is controlling?

Think of a time when you felt absolute joy and freedom. If you can't think of such a time, then invent it. Are you alone? With someone else? Describe how your body feels.

Glossary

Let's get on the same page. Following are some basic terms you'll hear a lot in nonmonogamous communities, as well as terms I'll be using throughout this book and in conversation with our polyam experts. And because no information is ever presented with 100 percent objectivity, I'll be giving my best, personal working definitions of concepts such as *polyamory*, *open relationships*, *relationship anarchy*, and more, as well as my opinion and two cents on these terms.

These are living definitions, open to change and new information. As you read through them, pay attention to which terms jump out at you and your immediate, gut reaction to them. These reactions may come from a place of excitement, interest, judgment, or disagreement. And that's fine! The point here is for us to speak the same language—and for you to get comfortable asking yourself and others, *What do we mean when we say this? Are we operating on actual understanding? Or on assumptions of understanding? How can I articulate exactly what I want and hope for when I use these words? What do these words mean to me, and how can I express this to myself and others?*

Accountability. You'll read this word a lot. Accountability means taking responsibility for your actions, acknowledging the harm you've caused, and making amends for your mistakes. Accountability is more than just an apology, because it demands changed behavior as well. We'll get into the basics of accountability in Section 2.

Compersion. Compersion is often described as the opposite of jealousy. But more specifically, compersion is the joy or contentment you feel when your partner is with another person. For example, if you feel excited that your partner just had a great date, that feeling may be described as compersion. There can be a lot of overemphasis on compersion; some folks may feel pressured to feel compersion all the time and for all their partners. Compersion is something that happens, and it's wonderful when it does, but it's not a be-all and end-all goal for nonmonogamous folks. Feeling bad, confused, or neutral is also a fine and normal response.

Consent. Consent is a voluntary, fully informed, and risk aware agreement. These three pieces of consent are very important, so I'll break them down. Consent must be voluntary, meaning no one is under pressure or duress to make any particular decision; to be voluntary means each person *genuinely* wants something to happen, be it sex or a relationship, and there are no consequences if they do *not* want it to happen. Consent should be fully informed, meaning everyone has all the information, knowledge, and context needed to make a voluntary decision.

And finally, consent should be risk aware, meaning someone is fully informed of potential risks and is able to decide what is best for them. For example, imagine you are going to have sex with someone, and they inform you that they've had unprotected sex recently. They also inform you that it's been three years since their most recent sexually transmitted infection (STI) test. You now have a better understanding of the potential risk that comes along with having sex with this person. You may decide to mitigate that risk with safer sex precautions or barrier methods, or you may decide to not have sex. Either way, you were risk aware and therefore better able to provide or decline consent.

Couple Privilege. Couple privilege describes the power dynamic established partnerships often have over other newer partners in relationships. There is nothing wrong with having a wonderful, stable, long-term partner. But it's important to remember how that affects new partners. This is especially important if group sex comes into play, especially threesomes. Talking about couple privilege is a call to make sure you mitigate, acknowledge, and prepare for power dynamics in order to protect all parties from unnecessary hurt, especially regarding consent—which we should all be doing anyway!

Don't Ask, Don't Tell. This is a common phrase for folks in open relationships and much less so for those in polyamorous relationships. "Don't ask, don't tell" (DADT) is exactly what it sounds like: partners can have sex with other people outside their relationship but can't ask or tell their partners about it. Typically, this type of nonmonogamy allows only for one-night stands and not for the development of intimacy. Safer sex should also be a consideration for DADT. If discussions of other lovers aren't "allowed," then how can you talk about STIs, testing, condom use, and so on?

Ethical. Being ethical is something we'll talk about a lot in this book, and I am separating this term into its own definition rather than tacking *nonmonogamy* onto it. The word demands its own space because not all relationships are ethical.

Being ethical is about respect, honesty, and advocacy. An ethical person, in the context of nonmonogamy, is one who advocates for their own freedom and safety, and the freedom and safety of others. Being ethical looks like being honest about your intentions, desires, and needs. It looks like educating yourself on consent, power, and safer sex, and getting into relationships only where all parties are *fully informed about and consenting to that relationship.*

Hard Feelings. I use this term a lot in my life. Hard Feelings can be hurt, confusion, anger, jealousy, or any combination of them. Sometimes Hard Feelings are a sign there is work to be done: communication, therapy, private time to be had, coping mechanisms to be used. At other times, Hard Feelings just mean that you're having a hard time and must allow yourself to feel your feelings rather than attempt to fix them.

Hierarchy. Some nonmonogamous folks structure their relationships through a hierarchy. Many will have one "primary" partner, with whom they spend most of their time and may share finances or cohabitate with. Then there are "secondary" and "tertiary" relationships. This method works well for some people, and many people new to polyamory will often structure their existing monogamous relationship as the primary, and then any new partners as secondary or tertiary.

But hierarchies can also be seen as a remnant of monogamy. I believe hierarchy works against the true nature of relationships, which are ever changing and ever evolving, and relies too heavily on control and allocation. What happens if you want a more serious relationship with a "secondary" partner? What happens if your partner wants to spend more time with another person? Hierarchy, in my opinion, often relies on a false sense of control over your partner and their feelings. People can't be boxed in.

Jealousy. Jealousy is one of the most talked-about topics in polyamory, and something I've been asked about on many occasions. *How do I deal with it? How do I stop it?* It's important to remember that jealousy is just an emotion. It is a powerful emotion, and it usually feels terrible. But when you feel this emotion, it's your body signaling distress, either real or imagined. In polyamory, it's important to have tools to deal with Hard Feelings and not let these emotions control you—or lead you to be controlling.

Kitchen Table Polyamory. Kitchen table polyamory describes a polycule, or network of lovers, where all parties feel comfortable sharing spaces together and all know one another. The idea is that all parties can sit at the same kitchen table, feel comfortable and welcomed, and share a meal or conversation.

Metamour. A metamour, also known as a "meta," is a term commonly used to describe the lover of your lover. Say your girlfriend has a boyfriend. That boyfriend is your metamour.

Nesting Mate. A nesting mate is someone you live with and are in an important relationship with. This term is often used as an alternative to *primary partner* for those who don't have hierarchies in their relationship, but still want to acknowledge financial, emotional, and cohabitation ties with another.

Nonmonogamy. This is a term used to describe consensual emotional, sexual, and romantic relationships between multiple people. There are many types of nonmonogamy, including polyamory, open relationships, and swinging, which are defined in this glossary. Just remember that not all nonmonogamy is the same: you should be asking and clarifying what people mean when they say "nonmonogamy," because some styles are far more ethical than others.

Open Relationship. An open relationship is a more informal style of nonmonogamy. Folks in open relationships can engage in intimate, sexual, or romantic relationships with more than one partner, but open relationships tend to centralize a "primary," or "main," partnership. Sometimes open relationships mean that primary partners can have sex with others outside the relationship, but only with no emotions, or "strings," attached. The specific parameters of open relationships depend on the partners and people involved, so it's *always* a good idea to clarify what folks mean when they say they are open.

Polyamory. Polyamory is a type of nonmonogamy where folks have intimate, sexual, or romantic relationships with more than one person.

Polycule. This describes a network of lovers. A polycule includes a person's relationships with partners and their wider connections to their metamours. So if you have a girlfriend and she has a boyfriend, you'd all be in the same polycule. Some people understand their polycule as their immediate and extended family, while others have very limited contact with some members.

Relationship Anarchy. This term was coined by queer feminist Andie Nordgren and describes a kind of ethical nonmonogamy based in abundance and relationship building (rather than just sex). I most align with the tenets of relationship anarchy (RA), because it is based on freedom, communication, and shared values. RA does not have set relationship structures, rules, or hierarchies, meaning each individual is able to grow, change, and nurture relationships of their own choosing. RA also acknowledges that significant, intimate relationships do not have to be sexual to matter deeply. Nordgren writes in *The Short Instructional Manifesto for Relationship Anarchy*, "Relationship anarchy is not about never committing to anything—it's about designing your own commitments with the people around you."

Safer Sex. Safer sex is about protecting you and your partners from STIs, and this is especially important in nonmonogamous communities. Safer sex looks different for everyone, but you should periodically discuss barrier methods, regular STI testing, and sex toy hygiene with your regular or potential sexual partners.

Solo Polyamory. Solo polyamory, or solo polyam, is the approach taken by people who are polyamorous but are currently single or not looking to enter serious, committed relationships.

Swinging. Swinging is a kind of relationship in which committed partners, often married, have sex with other committed or married couples. Couples may engage in group sex or "switch" partners. Swinging is a bit old school, usually just for recreational sex, and not always the most queer friendly—but every group is different.

Unicorn Hunters. Unicorn hunters are usually cis heterosexual couples looking for sex to fulfill a fantasy. I find unicorn hunting deeply unethical because it relies on the fetishization of (usually) queer or bisexual women. People are not sex toys. People are not fantasies.

Ethical nonmonogamy requires respect, negotiation, and acknowledgment of humanity. Group sex and group dating dynamics are perfectly reasonable wants and can be done ethically through informed consent, risk mitigation, and other strategies—but unicorn hunting is not that.

SECTION 1

THE BASICS OF ETHICAL NONMONOGAMY

Section 1 is all about introducing you to the main themes of polyamory, with an emphasis on how you may begin to find the place, language, relationships, and desires that speak to you. Here, we'll be exploring the internal world: the desires, questions, fears, and curiosity that may leave us interested in, but perhaps intimidated by, polyamory.

Chapter 1 consists of questions and answers with sexuality and relationship educator Sam, founder of the digital platform *Shrimp Teeth*. I talk with Sam about their work, their first exposure to polyamory, their mistakes, their pitfalls, and how they deal with all the big and Hard Feelings that may come along with acclimating to a nonmonogamous lifestyle. This is the first Q&A in the book because in our conversation, Sam discusses with honesty, humor, and compassion her experiences coming into her own through polyamory—a process we all have to go through and may revisit as our needs and relationships change.

In Chapter 2, "Approaching Polyam Relationships," I work my way through the main, and sometimes messy, concepts that will both support and challenge your relationship to polyamory. Power, control, and freedom are a big part of this section, as I relate it back to the core ethics of polyamory and ask, What even is polyamory? What isn't it? And, of course, what does it mean to me?

Then, in Chapter 3, I discuss the basics of approaching nonmonogamous relationships, the trials and errors of finding a dynamic or relationship style right for you, exploring new relationships with integrity and honesty, and the do's and don'ts of nonmonogamous relationships.

My intention isn't to overwhelm you with this section, or front-load you with a big neon sign that says "Polyamory is hard! There is trial and error! Breakups suck!" But neither is it my intention to tell you polyamory is easy. It's not.

Polyamory is hard because relationships are hard. And the more relationships you have, the more you must learn about yourself. Your habits. Your triggers. Your communication style. The ways you evade or deal with conflict. The ways you project, control, or are unrealistic.

Polyamory requires a humbleness of spirit, the strength to stick to your ideals, and the flexibility to change and adapt when you're getting in your own way. The more I do this, the more I learn from others and from myself. And as I think about what I want and value, and act in accordance with my values and with respect for the agency of others, the more realistic, free, and joyous my relationships are.

I ask you to keep an open mind as you read through this chapter, and keep a finger on the pulse of your emotions. Are you feeling excitement? Anxiety? Confidence? These emotions are all clues to your internal world and how you may relate to polyamory.

Take breaks as you move through this section, and spend time on the activities throughout it. The activities are here to help you process and identify parts of yourself and current or previous relationships that you'd like to strengthen, explore, change, or reframe.

Chapter 1

TALKING POLYAMORY WITH SAM OF *SHRIMP TEETH*

I first came across Sam—an artist, an educator, and the founder of the polyam and sexuality-focused platform *Shrimp Teeth*—via social media. As you read through our conversation, pay attention to the many ways people come across, and come into, ethical nonmonogamy.

SYG: Hi, Sam. I'm so excited to talk to you. I've been following your work for a few years now, but for those who don't know you, can you introduce yourself?

SAM: Hi, I'm Sam (she/they). I'm an artist, educator, and the founder of *Shrimp Teeth* (www .shrimpteeth.com), a digital platform that helps folks reclaim and explore their sexuality and relationships. *Shrimp Teeth* started as an Instagram account (@shrimpteeth) back in 2017 where I documented the process of opening my relationship. I had just moved cross-country, from New York to Portland, with my partner and suddenly met someone new, which forced us to dive headfirst into polyamory. It doesn't seem that long ago, but there were far fewer folks talking about ethical nonmonogamy, and it was challenging to find resources. My goal wasn't to create a business. I was simply making art about my polyam experience and using Instagram as a catalog. But within a few months, I had over 20,000 followers, and people were reaching out, asking me questions about ENM [ethical nonmonogamy].

My background is in design and consumer psychology. I knew right out of grad school that I didn't want to be a therapist, but I started playing around with the idea of applying con-psy ideas to relationship education. Basically, my philosophy is that we all have certain preferences when it comes to the ways we relate to other folks, and by offering a variety of options (that most people don't even know are available), I help individuals explore. I operate from a free-choice model: each individual has the right and responsibility to decide what forms of consensual intimacy and relationships they want to participate in. I avoid standardizing as much as possible because I recognize the wide range of human experiences.

To say that *all* humans must be in a monogamous, romantic, sexual cohabiting relationship for their entire adult life sounds just as ridiculous to me as saying that all humans should only eat pesto spaghetti for every meal for their entire lives! Unfortunately, when it comes to sex and relationships, we still believe there's a singular moral script. I reject that idea completely and encourage people to think critically. I've talked to folks about these topics ever since. I've done over 1,100 peer support sessions in the past couple years. And I now have a yearlong course that helps couples slowly develop relationship skills that help them navigate opening their relationship and troubleshooting some of the common issues that pop up.

SYG: Sam, let's just jump right in. I think the first time I actually read the word *polyamory*, I was on Reddit at maybe fifteen or sixteen years of age. I'd never dated anyone, never even been out on a date at that point, but I was interested in kind of alternative romantic situations. I remember reading this post about a woman whose husband was sleeping over at his girlfriend's house a few nights a week. *So many* people responded to the post and talked about similar arrangements they had with multiple partners. I was absolutely shocked. I remember it being a mixture of awe and some sort of judgmental disbelief. Like, *How could that possibly work*?

Tell me about the first time you heard about nonmonogamy. Where did you hear about it? What did you think? How old were you? Were you attracted to the idea?

SAM: Right off the bat, at fifteen years old, I started dating and sleeping with multiple people, and I never stopped. As you can imagine, I dealt with a lot of slut-shaming as a result. Still, I felt that monogamy was too restrictive but also didn't know that polyamory existed. That word wasn't on my radar until my mid-twenties. I started dating my buddy in high school, and he's been my platonic partner for over a decade. We had a pretty unusual arrangement from the start. I was casually seeing other people but felt a deep sense of loyalty to our friendship. To his credit, he's always supported the nonnormative parts of me and understood that traditional relationship norms wouldn't work.

We began a long-distance relationship during college; that's when I started sleeping more regularly with friends and tiptoeing into exploring my queerness. My buddy and I stumbled messily into nonmonogamy, backtracked, and fell into it again. I'm a bit of a slut, so monosexuality never seemed like a realistic option. I just didn't know other ethical options were possibilities at the time. We practiced Don't Ask, Don't Tell without having any formal guide until he moved in with me for grad school. The infidelity we'd justified due to long distance no longer worked, so we tried being monogamous for a stint. It became clearer to me during that time that I was gay and that monogamy was unrealistic as a result. As I mentioned, after moving to the Pacific Northwest and meeting someone else, we realized we had to get our shit together; we couldn't continue cheating forever. So I got a copy of *The Ethical Slut*, and we started planning how we would be honest with each other while incorporating other partners into our lives. It wasn't an easy transition.

SYG: What are some preconceived notions or beliefs folks have when they first realize their interest in polyamory? For me, I've noticed a lot of folks believe they can separate sex and emotions, or at least control their feelings by establishing hierarchies in their relationships (i.e., having primary, secondary, or tertiary partners). Then when folks get into relationships, they realize love and commitment is much messier, and can't always be neatly contained—especially as relationships and needs start to change and develop over time! My belief is that love and partnership resists rules, definitions, and hierarchy.

If you could go back in time and have a sit-down with your former self, what would you say? What are some of the preconceived notions you had, or that you come across in your work? What do you want folks who are just coming into polyamory to know and to challenge?

SAM: Most of my early experiences were trial and error. Nothing was very well thought out. I was going with my instinct, not realizing there was a plethora of resources available. Unfortunately, our standard relationship scripts hyper focus on finding a partner, and gloss over what happens after, or glorify toxic behavior patterns. None of us are perfect when it comes to love. However, it's important that we recognize that being in a relationship requires learning skills, putting energy into maintaining connections, and doing personal growth work. Obviously, I made a ton of mistakes starting out because, like many folks, I thought you could just *be* nonmonogamous. So often we underestimate the deliberate work involved in *practicing* polyam.

It took me awhile to grasp how much toxic/compulsory monogamy informed the way I viewed and practiced ENM. Comp-mono shows up everywhere! For example, I still struggle to let go of the fear that my meta will trick my partner into leaving me. Jealousy often stems from ownership myths that are reinforced by standard relationship scripts. I think, unfortunately, most of us haven't had opportunities to challenge cultural views of how relationships *should* be. It's hard to sustain multiple relationships with folks who have multiple relationships when deep down you believe you own your pals, that you need to be their everything, that you're entitled to each other's time and attention, etc. I wish I'd been more aware of how much cultural unlearning I would have to do. I don't believe that nonmonogamy is inherently superior to other relationship structures. However, it does force you to challenge the way we've been told to relate to others. That can be a frightening ask for many people.

As ENM grows in popularity, there's a slew of folks who assume they can just call themselves polyam and have loads of sex without further reflection. The hard reality is that more relationships means you have to do more relationship maintenance and more self-work. Not everyone is into that! From my peer support sessions, I've noticed there's a spectrum of folks who are opening up. On one end are people full of fear who don't really believe that ENM is possible. On the other end are folks who tend to be a bit careless (like me, initially!) and haven't taken the time to learn about ENM. Folks who fall somewhere in the middle tend to do better, because they understand that nonmonogamy requires a lot of small steps to unlearn years of comp-mono programming. The folks who I hear successfully sustain polyamory view opening up as a learning process rather than a way to acquire more sex, love, attention, etc.

SYG: For me, my biggest draw to polyamory wasn't endless, hot sex or eternal dating options. I knew I wanted a wider community of support, wisdom, and trust. For me, that looks like opening up what partnership and family means. My polyam network isn't just people I sleep with. In fact, I have really important, deeply loving relationships where sex *isn't* on the table. Polyamory is also about the elders I turn to for support, the lovers-of-my-lovers who I meet and bond with and share respect for, the metamours I work with to mutually support loved ones.

As a lesbian, I view polyamory as a way to create a family and wider network of mutual care and support. What's it like for you?

SAM: I separate my dating history into three major eras: starting with Don't Ask, Don't Tell in high school and college, moving into necessary polyamory after grad school, and currently landing in hybrid relationship anarchy. The way I view my relationships has evolved as a result. In the beginning, I was having casual sex with other people without talking about it. Nonmonogamy was purely focused on sex, and it frankly didn't touch other parts of my life. It wasn't fully secret, but I never dreamed of publicly identifying as ENM. When I "officially " became polyamorous, it was out of necessity to resolve a sexual incongruence with my buddy.

At the time, I had realized that I was gay (instead of bi), and neither he nor I wanted to be celibate. My buddy and I returned to a platonic arrangement and made space to date other people; our girlfriends were secondary, in the sense that he and I shared the bulk of our resources. At the time, he and I were intent on remaining primary life partners. Then Covid happened and sent all our plans to shit; we ended up separating and I moved in with one of my girlfriends. Due to the threats posed by the pandemic as well as living with someone who identifies as monogamous, I've had to yet again reexamine what ENM means to me.

As it stands, my polyamorous practice focuses more on family building. My buddy and I are still friends even if we are no longer primary life partners, my girlfriend and I U-hauled[1] and became far more focal in each other's lives than we'd ever anticipated, and the other person I was dating has become my qupee (a bastardization of queer platonic relationship) but dates separately. Somehow my girlfriend and qupee have managed to resolve initial jealousy, and we have something that resembles a Kitchen Table Polyamory structure now. From the outside, it's hard to explain to folks what is nonmonogamous about our arrangement. But I can tell you for certain that people who I used to date wouldn't occupy the space in my life to the extent they [my buddy and my qupee] do if we were in a typical monogamous structure.

I'm currently dipping for the first time into a deliberately monosexual relationship, which has been both challenging and lovely. It's forcing me, for the first time in my life, to expand my sexual curiosity with a single person rather than relying on multiple people to provide variety. But I've learned that I can' t expect to stay consistent forever; I 'm always open to the change that will inevitably happen. While sex now occupies a smaller part of my polyam practice, the way I think about love and the possibilities for connections has expanded. When I say I'm a hybrid relationship anarchist, I mean that I see each of my pals as unique individuals who are able to define boundaries and agreements. I want my relationships to be special and authentic rather than forcing us into predefined structures. I have a lot more flexibility and freedom in how I relate to others as a result.

SYG: Over the past seven or eight years of practicing ethical nonmonogamy, I've gotten a lot better at being realistic about my time and energy. At first, I was willing to try any partnership and go out on any date. Now, I'm a lot more measured in how willing I am to approach new relationships, because I realize with every new relationship, there's always a learning curve for how that will affect me, the other person, and the equilibrium of not just my life but my polycule's lives. I spend more time reflecting about the energy I can give to others. I also spend a lot more time vetting other folks: Are we truly compatible? What are the expectations here? Are they realistic and what if they change? Are we speaking

---

1 *U-hauled* is a term used primarily in lesbian communities that describes the phenomenon of meeting someone and moving in together very, very quickly.

the same language when it comes to what we want from polyamory, or what we even mean when we say *polyamory*?

How have your needs and expectations for polyamory shifted over time? How do you decide when you're ready for a new relationship? What should folks think about as they approach polyam relationships?

SAM: Possibly the biggest shift in my practice has been slowing down. I describe myself as an "itchy" person, meaning that I'm quickly bored and always looking for the next interesting experience or person. Unfortunately, I've learned this attitude is a recipe for chaos: I've gotten quickly oversaturated and I've dated a bunch of people who weren't actually cool with ENM. Looking back at the earlier years, I see clearly how I've hurt a lot of my exes' feelings also by moving too fast, not taking enough time to clarify expectations, and bringing people with lots of weird baggage into the established polycule. I absolutely adore my current partners, so I've been mindful when the itchy feeling pops up to take a deep breath, rather than make spontaneous plans or go on a bunch of dates.

I've also dated a few people who confused the terms *ENM* and *dating*, meaning they were seeing multiple people but with the intention of settling down with one. I think as ENM becomes a more popular term, this is becoming a larger issue, which makes it really hard to find folks who are on the same page. There's no problem with dating and wanting to find a monogamous partner, but that's not the same as being polyamorous. I'm much more mindful of this issue now than I was initially.

I've seen the relationship between my nesting partner and qupee flourish over the past two years, and it makes me realize how much I value cohesion. I have no patience for folks who use ENM as a way to audition partners for eventual monogamy. I'm no longer willing to be at odds with, or kept in the dark about, my metamours. In that way, I've become more protective of my existing polycule. I only bring in folks who want to build community with us. I try really hard not to restrict or create rules. However, I only want to date people who align with our existing values. Folks who want to be vague, not adhere to safer sex practices, or use us as sexual experiments for their queerness aren't the right fit. I try to see this as a compatibility issue rather than shame those folks. Just because those behaviors don't align with my preferences and values doesn't mean that's true for everyone. If I'm incompatible with someone, that's okay. There's eight billion people that could be a better fit.

SYG: Discomfort can be a big part of the polyam experience, no matter if you're a veteran or newbie to nonmonogamy. What would you say to folks who are nervous or anxious about dealing with conflict, jealousy, or the unknown? Can you share a time you were uncomfortable, jealous, or in conflict? What did you do? How did you find support? What were your coping mechanisms?

SAM: ENM made me confront the fact that I needed to learn how to examine and explain my emotions. It also made me unearth codependent tendencies with my buddy. Just because we refuse to critically examine how we engage with others doesn't mean our relationships are devoid of problems. I've noticed that ENM shines a light on existing problems, but it doesn't necessarily create new ones. When people struggle to deal with jealousy, it indicates that they haven't learned the skills to address it yet. As I mentioned earlier, being polyamorous requires us to acknowledge that we're constantly learning. When I opened up, I experienced jealousy that felt entirely unmanageable because I had never had to manage it before. Mastering some DBT [dialectical behavioral therapy] skills for emotional regulation and distress tolerance was super useful for dealing with spicy emotions. Similarly, developing a shared language with my buddy to communicate our boundaries and agreements allowed us to navigate conflict in ways we'd never done before.

People often (wrongly) assume that monogamy is easier. And while monogamy is certainly more socially and culturally normalized, it doesn't necessarily mean it's simpler. Everyone at some point needs to learn how to communicate, how to deal with difficult emotions, how to resolve conflict. ENM often prompts us to look for solutions to problems that already exist. Still, none of this is easy. Once I'd come to terms with the areas I needed to strengthen, I still had to learn those skills. And everyone goes through a different process of learning.

For me personally, learning these skills happened by creating activity sheets, templates, and workbooks. I would examine the problems I was facing from a detached perspective, and create outlines that I thought would be helpful for myself and my pals. The bulk of the content you see on *Shrimp Teeth* are tools that I originally developed for personal use. I realized through peer support sessions that most people opening their relationships were struggling with similar issues, so I made all this content available to others. But at the end of the day, it's important to find what works for you as an individual.

It's foolish to think you can jump into a new endeavor without some sort of learning curve. ENM is no different. It's tricky at first because you're facing completely new situations, with very little skills and lots of fear. It does progressively get easier. The trick is having enough resilience and compassion to endure the initial phases.

SYG: In this book, I talk a lot about control and freedom, and how those two forces inform our relationships. What is your personal definition of freedom? What does a free relationship look like to you? How does it feel? When do you know you're in a relationship that prioritizes freedom?

SAM: Both freedom and control are responses to fear. When faced with uncertainty (for example, about how our relationship will change after introducing a new partner), we are left with the option to let go or to buckle down. This also plays into the difference between a scarcity and an abundance mindset. In a scarcity headspace, you're competing with everyone else for perceived limited resources. The fear that you won't get enough results in a desire for control. You end up trying to restrict other people so you can gain the most access to your pals' love, time, attention, etc. Folks who give in to their fear establish rigid rules, hold couple privilege over others, and have a generally defensive attitude toward metas.

In an abundance mindset, you're able to recognize that constraints are about perspective. Fear is subsided by zooming out and letting go of entitlement. You give each other the freedom to choose when and how you allocate resources, knowing there will always be more opportunities to share love, time, attention, etc.

Yes, time is limited if you focus on the limitation. For example, if you want a date on Friday night with your pal, but they're already going on a date with someone else, in a scarcity framework you will fight for your right to that specific day and insist your pal choose you over your meta. You exert control as a way to resolve your fear that you're not important to your pal. In an abundance framework, given the same situation, you're able to zoom out and realize there are endless Fridays. You give your pals and yourself the freedom to make plans with other people, realizing it doesn't take away the inherent value and quality of your relationship. Your pal choosing to spend time with someone else doesn't mean they don't want to be with you. In response to the fear of not being a priority, you might ask your partner to plan something on a day they are available. Freedom comes from these mindset shifts, but they take time to integrate.

Speaking personally, I get really bogged down by my initial fear response. My impulse is to tell my metas and pals what to do in order to reduce change. I will say that it's not a conscious process. I'm prone to what I call "creative jealousy," conjuring vivid fear-based fantasies that cause additional distress. So it's really important to realize what's going on in my head and separate my spicy emotions from the actions and agreements I have with my pals. I do this by journaling every day. I write out my creative jealousy scenarios and vent out my anxieties. I go back through what I've written, redacting the scarcity mindset or the thoughts rooted in toxic comp-mono. I then force myself to rewrite the scenario from an ENM-friendly abundance mindset.

This practice trains my brain to let go of control and find the freedom I crave in my relationships. I want my pals to have rich and vivid lives that they can share with a variety of people. I'm also struggling against two decades of ingrained scarcity frameworks about love. Unlearning all the garbage takes time and deliberate practice.

Chapter 2

APPROACHING POLYAM RELATIONSHIPS

There's no one "right" way to do polyamory. Everyone comes into their nonmonogamous desires and commitments in different ways and under different circumstances. Maybe you're like me and for a long time felt that monogamy didn't quite fit. Maybe it's your partner who is talking about opening your relationship and you are doing some research. Maybe you have been polyam for a while now but feel the need to reset your expectations and habits in relationships.

Whatever your walk of life, having solid guiding principles will help you evaluate conflict, difficult conversations, and opportunities in an honest and realistic way.

Following are five concepts that guide my polyamorous practice. Each of these concepts I've learned through my seven-plus years of trial and error. I share them with you now for your polyam toolkit.

Polyam Toolkit

1. Be Honest

This is the first, and simplest, tenet of my polyamorous practice. Be honest. Don't lie to yourself or others. Be absolutely clear—paint a picture in detail—about who you are and what you're looking for.

Talk to your partners and potential partners about your experience with nonmonogamy, your current partnerships, and what you want from a relationship (sex? dating? casual? serious? platonic?). Describe exactly what this relationship looks like. Share with partners and potential partners what you're working on personally and in regard to relationships, challenges you have, support you may need, your sexual health, specifics about what safer sex means and looks like to you, the time and energy you have to dedicate to the relationship, and what a good, supportive relationship looks like to you.

Then ask your potential or current partner to discuss these same issues. The point here is to see if your desires and values and those of the other person's are compatible.

Taking the time to have these types of conversations lets people know where you stand. It allows you to think more critically about what you *actually* want versus going along with what someone else wants because you're not sure.

It's also worth mentioning that honesty, like consent, has a reputation for "killing the mood" or " being unsexy." But this misses the point. Spending time together doesn't have to be sexy to be enjoyable or intimate to be important. Sexiness is ephemeral—but the trust and connection you build via honesty are not.

2. Don't Assume Others Understand You

People want to be understood, but it takes time and effort to connect the dots between what you want versus what you *think* you want. What you said versus how it was understood. What you feel versus what others think you feel.

This is why clarifying questions are so important. When you're in conversation with someone, ask questions and confirm understanding. I'll give you an example.

> Three partners are having a check-in about their relationship. Jessica and Andi have been together for three years, and about a year ago Jessica and Charlotte started dating. All three have a regular check-in once a month or so, and today they're talking about the possibility of Charlotte moving into the extra bedroom of Jessica and Andi's house.

Jessica: So the house has three bedrooms. Andi and I usually sleep together three nights a week, but I generally like to sleep alone at least twice a week.

Andi: We don't really have a set schedule about when we spend the night together. Typically, we just ask the other person sometime during the day or before bed if they want company that night. On average, it works out to about three or so nights, but sometimes if I have to work early or I get home late, I prefer sleeping alone. And if my partner from out of state comes to visit, I'll spend those consecutive nights with them.

Charlotte: Okay, that makes sense.

Andi, Jessica, and Charlotte then move on to discuss rent and other aspects of living together.

This might look like a great conversation. There's nothing *wrong* with this conversation, but there are no built-in affirmations of true understanding.

Andi may walk away from this conversation assuming that Jessica and Charlotte will work out between the two of them what nights they will spend together, but Andi will still expect to sleep with Jessica three or so nights a week as usual. Jessica may walk away feeling a little stressed about managing to get her two solo nights in every week but feel good enough to move on, assuming that both Andi and Charlotte will ask before bedtime what she's down for. Charlotte may walk away thinking that she and Andi will each get two guaranteed nights a week with Jessica.

Let's redo this conversation so that, rather than making assumptions, each person takes the time to make sure they are understood.

Jessica: So the house has three bedrooms. Andi and I usually sleep together three nights a week, but I generally like to sleep alone at least twice a week.

Charlotte: Okay, just so I'm clear, you need two nights alone every week? Or does it just depend on your schedule? Or how you're feeling?

Jessica: Thanks for asking. I need Monday and Wednesday nights alone every week. I get up at 7 a.m. on Tuesdays and Thursdays to work out. So I need to get a good night's sleep. And I just really need the alone time.

Charlotte: Okay, that makes total sense. So Monday and Wednesday nights are your time.

Andi: We don't really have a set schedule about when we spend the night together, other than not having Monday or Wednesday nights together. Typically, we just ask the other person sometime during the day or before bed if they want company that night. On average, it works out to about three or so nights, but sometimes if I have to leave for work early or I get home late, I prefer sleeping alone. And if my partner from out of state comes to visit, I'll spend those consecutive nights with them. When my partner visits, I'll let you both know ahead of time to make sure the timing works out, and I always put the dates on the calendar in the kitchen too.

Jessica: Now with Charlotte potentially moving in, I'm not sure how realistic three or so nights a week is anymore. Charlotte and I were thinking maybe one or two nights a week together. What do you think about that?

Andi: Oh, okay. I was thinking we'd still have the three nights, so I probably need to readjust those expectations. I definitely want us to have that quality time, but I can be flexible. What do you two think about having a schedule?

Charlotte: I really like the idea of doing check-ins about sleeping together. I'd prefer that to a specific sleeping schedule because my work schedule always looks different from week to week, and I could bring someone home on a weekend or something.

Andi: Okay, so what I'm hearing is you don't want a schedule but rather just a see-how-we-feel situation?

Charlotte: Yeah, exactly. But I'm not sure where that leaves Jessica. I don't want her to feel stressed about managing all the check-ins or feel pressured to spend

X number of nights with us. What would a good check-in system look like for you, Jessica?

Jessica: A good check-in for me would look like _____.

So in the second conversation, each person seeks affirmations of understanding. Andi's assumption that he will get three or so nights a week is addressed, and he readjusts his expectations. Their conversation becomes longer and more detailed as each person works out exactly what a good sleeping situation would look like and honors Jessica's stated boundary: two nights alone. By taking the time to ask what a good check-in looks like, Charlotte is better able to understand the most efficient, least stressful way to communicate with Jessica, adapt, and modify Andi and Jessica's preestablished dynamic, while feeling she has the agency to bring home other partners or hookups as she wants.

In this conversation, everyone leaves the table with a *true* understanding, not an *assumed* understanding.

3. Be Humble

Being polyamorous is a lifelong learning process. As you move through relationships, you'll learn new things about yourself and others. You'll identify where you struggle to cope, realize where you need more support, and learn about new tools to help you and your partners navigate life.

I've been polyam for more than seven years, and have been educating myself on nonmonogamy for more than ten years total. I've had as many as five partners at a time, and sometimes no partner at all. I've moved with partners, cohabited with multiple partners at a time, watched my partners date others, slept with friends, gone through breakups, and been broken up with. Even after all that, I still don't feel like I'm an expert in polyamory. My goal is to *never* feel like an expert.

Overconfidence can leave you less adaptable and much more rigid than is good for you. Overconfidence sounds like, *I know how to do this. I know the right and only way to do this. This is what I know will happen.* Overconfidence looks like having huge blind spots concerning your own shortcomings, without the tools or self-awareness to address them.

You'll also notice that overconfidence leaves very little room for anyone else's opinions or needs. Overconfidence includes an assumption of understanding it *all*.

Humbleness, on the other hand, leaves you adaptable, open, and creative. Humbleness says, I am willing to work with you. I am willing to try something new. I am willing to cocreate a relationship. I am willing to learn.

Cultivate humbleness—the ability to receive new information and collaborate with others—in your relationships. Overconfidence is rigidity, but humbleness is not the same as malleability. You still need to know your values and boundaries, and you still need to be realistic about who your partners are and whether you and they are truly well suited for collaboration.

4. Manage Your Expectations

Expectations are the death of freedom. If that sounds harsh, then let me explain.

At their core, expectations are the beliefs that someone *should* or *must* do something. We put expectations on ourselves and others all the time, even without realizing it.

Some expectations are explicitly communicated, negotiated, and consented to by all parties involved. In fact, many expectations can be healthy. *I expect you to be honest with me. I expect you to accept my no the first time. I expect you to deal with conflict without yelling. I expect you to respect my decision to use a condom. I expect you to give me room to change and grow, and I expect to give you the same.*

But some expectations are assumed, meaning they are never communicated or negotiated. I expect to always be your first priority. I expect that you won't fall in love with anyone I don't like. I expect that we will never break up. I expect you to meet all my needs. I expect my relationships to always look one way. I expect you to never change.

Healthy expectations represent consensual agreements. Unhealthy expectations are a mechanism of control and a fast track to disappointment. To save yourself and others heartache, you first need to take a look in the mirror. Confront the parts of yourself that seek to control and limit others. Ask, *Is this fair to expect? Is this reasonable? Is this controlling? Is this ego-driven, or freedom-seeking? How would I feel if someone held this expectation of me?*

Then you need to talk about your expectations in depth, not only with yourself but also with your partners. Your expectations must be made explicit, so that all parties are fully informed and consenting.

5. Walk the Walk and Talk the Talk

As you journey into different polyam communities, you'll find a lot of different people. Some will be amazing, fascinating people. Others will rub you the wrong way and make that little voice in your head say, *Run.*

The most important piece of advice I can give you is this: pay attention to what people do, not what they say.

Some people will know all the right words: *ethical, Kitchen Table Polyamory, accountability, communication,* and so on. They may impress you with the way they talk, the concepts they're familiar with, or the fact that they've read a million books on polyamory or relationship anarchy you've never even heard of. They may have the best politics or the coolest, most down-to-earth ideals. And this person may still be an absolute asshole and a misery to date because they don't actually *do* the things they say they do.

I once dated someone who talked endlessly about accountability. This person had plans for the best way to repair relationships. They had an explanation and a story for every time someone had treated them badly and how the offending party had failed to be accountable. Yet when this partner caused me true, real hurt, they were completely unable to apologize or make meaningful behavioral changes. They dismissed me. They blamed me. They blamed their upbringing. They blamed my other partners. They promised to change their behavior a million times. I chose to believe their words and ignore their actions. Nothing changed, and each time I got hurt worse, until I finally had enough.

Beware of this type of person. And, as Maya Angelou said, when they show you who they are, believe them the first time.

Look for people whose actions align with their words. And strive to *be* a person whose ideals and values show up in the way they treat others, disclose important information, own up to their mistakes, make amends, and enforce realistic boundaries.

THE DO'S AND DON'TS OF POLYAMORY

- DO prioritize your freedom.
- DO prioritize and respect your partners' agency.
- DO assume others have good intentions.
- DO adopt an "us versus the problem" mentality.

- DON'T control your partner via rules, double standards, or guilt trips.
- DON'T rely on rule-making to avoid your own discomfort.
- DON'T expect others to save you, parent you, or fix you.

THE DO'S AND DON'TS OF POLYAMORY

- DO check your ego.
- DO interrogate double standards.
- DO interrogate the ways sexism, racism, white supremacy, ableism, sex negativity, and homophobia may show up in your relationships.
- DO take responsibility for your actions.
- DO learn the difference between healthy and unhealthy expectations.
- DO let go of unhealthy expectations.
- DO learn how to apologize well.
- DO approach your metamours with curiosity and warmth.
- DO get tested regularly for STIs.
- DO get comfortable talking about sex— and get educated.
- DO get comfortable acknowledging and identifying areas in yourself where personal growth is needed.
- DO get used to asking people for support.
- DO get used to asking, How can I support you right now?
- DO use boundaries to protect yourself, not punish others.
- DO internalize that love is abundant.
- DO move away from a scarcity mentality and toward an abundance mentality.
- DO actively seek out tools, therapy, and education on ethical nonmonogamy.
- DO embrace change.

- DON'T compete with your partners for love and attention.
- DON'T make your discomfort other people's responsibility.
- DON'T compare yourself with other polyam people.
- DON'T compare yourself with your partner's partners.
- DON'T be hostile to your metamours.
- DON'T sabotage your partners' relationships.
- DON'T use polyamory to save a dying relationship.
- DON'T use polyamory as an excuse to do whatever you want.
- DON'T force a relationship open if not all parties are 100 percent onboard.
- DON'T use polyamory as an excuse to cheat.
- DON'T use other human beings as a fetish, experiment, or trial.
- DON'T assume polyamory makes you better than monogamous people.
- DON'T jump into polyamory if you don't know yourself. Figure out your own shit so that you don't drag others into it.
- DON'T assume that love is finite.
- DON'T be afraid of change.
- DON'T judge yourself for experiencing a learning curve.

Let's Check In

You've read a *ton* of information. Take a few minutes to check in with yourself. How is your body feeling? What emotions are you feeling? Can you name them?

Once you've settled into the moment, gather your thoughts. Write down your answers to the questions that follow. Be honest with yourself! There are no right or wrong answers. The point is to better understand yourself, your desire for polyamory, and your capacity for success in polyamory.

Why are you interested in polyamory?

What motivates you to explore polyamory?

What are your strengths as a partner? What's your plan to develop these strengths further?

What are your strengths as a communicator? What's your plan to develop these strengths further?

What are your weaknesses as a partner? What's your plan to improve these weaknesses?

What are your weaknesses as a communicator? What's your plan to improve these weaknesses?

What are some challenges you've experienced or expect to experience with polyamory? How will you address them? Paint the picture in detail.

Would you date yourself? Why or why not?

Chapter 3

MAKING THE SWITCH FROM A MONOGAMOUS TO A POLYAMOROUS MINDSET

Polyamory doesn't just require you to learn a new way of being in community and relationships: it also requires you to investigate and unlearn the monogamy you were taught. I was taught monogamy was the only correct way to love and be respectable. Therefore I learned many other, deeply rooted ideas that were never what I wanted: You can truly love only one person at a time. Marriage should be your goal, especially if you're a woman. Jealousy is a sign of love.

Polyamory forced me to address my socialization regarding monogamy, and how it interacted with other systems of power and belief. Don't get me wrong. Monogamy is not inherently bad, just like polyamory is not inherently good or a more enlightened relationship style. But the way monogamy is taught and often drilled into people's heads says a lot about power, sexism, classism, homophobia, purity culture, and sex negativity.

For example, a cis man may come into polyamory thinking that if his girlfriend sleeps with another man, he will not be "man enough" for his girlfriend or others. He may act out to save face. Some people may feel guilt or shame for being " promiscuous" and limit their own sexual freedom. Others come to polyamory thinking that STIs make people "dirty" or undesirable. You may see a disabled person thriving with their partners and think, *Who would want to date* them? As you move through relationships, make note of these times when your social conditioning reveals itself. Then question these ingrained beliefs, compare them with your own values, and educate yourself in the hope of doing better.

Making the switch from a monogamous to a polyamorous mindset can take a lot of time and patience—and that's why I love making charts. Charts are clear and helpful because complex ideas are presented in a simpler, more digestible way. Take a look at the chart that follows. I added in a few ideas to get you started. Finish filling out the chart. Then expand it!

Monogamous Mindset	Polyamorous Mindset
Love is finite.	Love is infinite.
	It's unrealistic to think my partner should or can meet all my needs.
	Jealousy is a sign I need to sit with my discomfort, self-soothe, and seek support.
My partner completes me.	
If my partner flirts with or loves someone else, then I'm not enough for them.	
Relationships should be restrictive.	Relationships should be expansive.

Monogamous Mindset	Polyamorous Mindset
I am entitled to my partner's time when I want or need it.	
My partner isn't allowed to do this or that.	
Sex is one of the most important parts of a romantic relationship.	
	My partners have a right to pleasure, freedom, and safety with other consenting adults.
Cheating looks like my partner experiencing emotional intimacy or having sex with anyone other than me.	

The Polyamory Workbook

Unhealthy versus Healthy Expectations

Take a look at each unhealthy expectation that follows. Think about why they might be unhealthy, controlling, or unrealistic. Then rewrite each expectation so that it's healthier.

Polyamory will be easy for me.

If I'm uncomfortable, insecure, or jealous, then I need to make rules for my relationships.

When I am uncomfortable, someone else must help me through this.

I'll always get along with my metamours.

My partners will always prioritize my needs.

I will always be available to meet my partners' needs.

My partners will always understand me. Because my partners understand me, they'll see things my way.

If my partner tells me they're looking to date casually, then they'll never change their mind or fall in love.

My partner will always tell me all the details of what's going on in their other relationships.

I have a say in how my partner develops their other relationships.

My partner and I will never break up.

‑‑‑

‑‑‑

Scarcity and Abundance

Recall my earlier conversation with Sam. She spoke about the differences between a scarcity and an abundance mindset.

In a scarcity mindset, "you're competing with everyone else for perceived limited resources. The fear is that you won't get enough results in a desire for control. You end up trying to restrict other people so you can gain the most access to your pals' love, time, attention, etc. Folks who give in to their fear establish rigid rules, hold couple privilege over others, and have a generally defensive attitude toward metas."

In an abundance mindset, "you're able to recognize that constraints are about perspective. Fear is subsided by zooming out and letting go of entitlement. You give each other the freedom to choose when and how you allocate resources, knowing there will always be more opportunities to share love, time, attention, etc."

Together, we're going to try out the journaling activity Sam mentioned. Write down a situation that scares you and activates your scarcity mindset. Write out all your fears, worst-case scenarios, and controlling impulses.

Then write about that same situation from an abundance mindset.

I've included an example to get things started. The scarcity narrative here might seem a bit over the top—but it's not. Most times, when we spiral, we spiral hard. Things that might look ridiculous on the page seem completely reasonable in a moment of distress.

Let go of entitlement, fear, paranoia, and defensiveness, and lean into freedom.

Situation: Your partner June is going away for the week to see their other partner Maria.

Scarcity: June is going away to see Maria, and I'm worried that June is going to have a great time without me. If they have a great time, then June will probably want to see Maria even more than they do now. Probably June and Maria will get even more serious, and then I won't be as important to June.

I'm not as sexy, fun, or smart as Maria. June loves Maria more than me. I think Maria must be trying to steal June away from me.

I'm going to make June call me every morning and night. I'll also need to know if they have sex and how often. I'm going to tell June that she can have weeklong visits only once every few months.

Abundance: June is going away for a week to see Maria. I'm feeling a little worried that I'll get lonely or jealous, but these are normal responses and I plan to see friends, stay busy, enjoy some alone time, and call my therapist if needed. June and I have spent many wonderful weeks together recently, so I understand why they're taking the time to see Maria. I also understand that it's realistic that Maria and June will want to have sex. If I were in that situation, so would I! I enjoy sex and I want my loved ones to have the freedom to do the same.

Before June leaves, I'll check in with them and see if and how we'll stay in touch during their trip. I would definitely like to know that they get to the airport and Maria's house safely, but other than that it's important that June enjoy her time without feeling like she has to call me all the time.

Situation:

Scarcity:

Abundance:

Situation:

Scarcity:

Abundance:

Situation:

Scarcity:

Abundance:

Chapter 4

HARD FEELINGS AND HOW WE REACT TO THEM

When I first started having conversations with my partner Salomé about sex, relationships, and consent, I struggled. A lot. When I felt overwhelmed, unsure, or confused, my first reaction was to shut down and ice out my loved ones. Salomé would ask, "What's going on in your head? Can you tell me what you're thinking about? Can you name your emotions?"

We tried using a feelings chart so I could look at it and identify my core emotions. Was I angry—or feeling insecure? Was I sad—or was it more accurate to say I felt lonely? What exactly did I mean when I said I felt bad?

The feelings chart was agony for me. *I didn't know how I felt.* I couldn't describe my feelings to myself, let alone someone else. I knew I was feeling big things—lots of things—but I couldn't put them into words. So I cut and ran. I shut down during conversations, and I left my loved ones to deal with the fallout of unresolved conflict or abandoned conversations without my contribution or support. After a while, I'd just say I was fine and nothing was wrong—which wasn't true—rather than go through the agony of trying to express myself.

Then, weeks after a conflict, I'd realize, *Oh yes. I was insecure.* Or, *Oh yes, that feeling was loneliness.* But these realizations were as frustrating as they were helpful. They also left Salomé feeling crazy because I'd go to such lengths to try to conceal what was so obviously there.

With the help of books, my therapist, Salomé, and other partners, I began accepting that not only was I *very* conflict avoidant, but also that I needed more tools to stay present during conflict and activating situations. I wanted the ability to acknowledge and communicate my emotions rather than deny them—even if I still needed time to figure out exactly what I was feeling.

Rather than working against my natural inclinations, we started trying to find ways for me to honor my need for lots of processing time, but not lie or misrepresent myself.

After a while, Salomé and I came up with a name for these challenging emotions: Hard Feelings.

What Are Hard Feelings?

Hard feelings are emotions that take us out of our *window of tolerance*. The window of tolerance is a concept presented by Dan Siegel, a clinical professor of psychiatry, in his 1999 book *The Developing Mind*.

When we're in our window of tolerance, we are able to thrive and function. We can think clearly. We have the ability to be adaptable, grounded, and receptive to new ideas and different opinions. We are able to connect with others.

But when we're out of our window of tolerance, our connection with others is severed. Most people go one of two ways: hypoarousal or hyperarousal.

If you're like me, then you fall on the side of hypoarousal. You go numb and shut down. You may lose track of time. You might feel ashamed or depressed. You may say half-formed thoughts that are unintentionally hurtful or nonsensical. You may struggle to find words, speak at all, or move your body normally.

If you're like Salomé, then you tend to get hyperaroused. You get anxious and full of energy. You may have outbursts. You may want to lean into the conflict, hoping to resolve it immediately. You may say things you don't mean or lash out.

Nothing good ever comes from a conversation when you or your loved ones are out of the window of tolerance. It's not a good time to talk or make decisions.

Hard Feelings are the emotions that make us leave our window of tolerance. The term *Hard Feelings* is purposefully vague because when we're leaving our window of tolerance, it's nearly impossible to think clearly or express ourselves with accuracy.

Hard Feelings are sometimes so large that they take up our entire capacity to function normally.

Hard Feelings can come from two places: external stimuli or internal stimuli.

External Stimuli

External stimuli are everything that happens to us that we can't control, but that affect our circumstances and emotions. Two examples follow. The first represents a reaction of hyperarousal and the second of hypoarousal.

Hyperarousal: You go to the doctor's office and get some bad news. Then, as you're leaving the doctor's office, your car won't start. You wait two hours for a jump, and you finally get home late. You feel frazzled, agitated, and completely overwhelmed. Your partner greets you and says something to you about doing the dishes. You lose it and start sobbing and yelling.

You're out of your window of tolerance due to external circumstances.

Hypoarousal: You and your partner have planned a special anniversary date, and you're both thrilled about it. You're attending the concert of your favorite artist, who rarely visits your city. The day of the event, your partner calls you: an emergency has come up at work and they have to miss the concert. They ask if they can still sleep over as planned and you agree. For the rest of the day, you feel sad, empty, and disappointed, but you try to pull yourself together. Your partner comes over that night very late, having just left the office. They apologize profusely but your feelings overwhelm you. You shut down, ice them out, and tell them to leave.

You're out of your window of tolerance due to external circumstances.

Internal Stimuli

Internal stimuli represent the thoughts and perceptions we have that affect our emotional well-being. Internal stimuli can be related to external stimuli but not always. Sometimes our thoughts just have a life of their own, and they can take us out of our window of tolerance. Read the two examples that follow.

Hyperarousal: You're having a terrible nightmare. You dream your partner has been hiding things from you and then breaks up with you out of nowhere. When you wake up, you're sweaty and upset. Your partner kisses you on the forehead and asks what's wrong. You snap and say something you don't mean. You pick a fight for no reason, and afterward feel insecure and embarrassed but also deeply annoyed with your partner.

You're out of your window of tolerance due to internal circumstances.

Hypoarousal: You and your partner July have been dating for six months. You're still fairly new to polyamory and haven't yet met July's other partner, Becca. July hasn't been pushy about the two of you meeting, but after six months you've decided you'd really like to meet Becca. July schedules a relaxed meeting at a coffee shop for later that week, excited for the two of you to meet. You arrive at the coffee shop, and July and Becca are there waiting for you. Becca greets you warmly and you're feeling pretty good, maybe a little hesitant and shy. July smiles at you, kisses Becca quickly, and welcomes you.

Suddenly you feel extremely uncomfortable. You hated seeing July kiss someone else. When July doesn't kiss you as well, you feel sure it means something. You try to get through the conversation, but you're convincing yourself that July meant the kiss to be a snub. You start imagining July having sex with Becca, and your jealousy feels out of control. You say next to nothing, sweat, and feel disconnected from July and hostile toward Becca. After, July tries to talk to you. You say that you're fine. But everything feels ruined.

You're out of your window of tolerance due to internal circumstances.

ACTIVITY

My Window of Tolerance

Window of Tolerance

Now let's take some time to reflect on how you handle your Hard Feelings and how you tend to act when in and out of your window of tolerance.

How do I define Hard Feelings? How do I feel when I have them?

How often am I in my window of tolerance? How often do I leave it?

Do I tend to get hyperaroused? Do I have a loved one who tends to get hyperaroused? What does this look like?

Do I tend to get hyporaroused? Do I have a loved one who tends to get hyporaroused? What does this look like?

When was the most recent time I was out of my window of tolerance? What happened? What did I do?

When was the most recent time I witnessed a loved one out of their window of tolerance? What happened? What did I do?

When have external stimuli triggered my Hard Feelings?

When have internal stimuli triggered my Hard Feelings?

When I have Hard Feelings, how do I comfort myself? How do others around me try to comfort me?

What's something I wish my loved ones knew about my Hard Feelings?

How to Use Hard Feelings

Hard Feelings are just that: big, unruly, difficult, and overwhelming. Hard Feelings may feel like a problem, but they aren't something we need to "fix." Rather, Hard Feelings are something we need to *listen to*.

If we're open, then we can hear our feelings tell us when we are out of or leaving our window of tolerance. They tell us when we need to slow down and self-soothe.

Hard feelings are actually really loud when you know what to listen for. They sound like, *I'm not okay. I need help. I need space to process. I need soothing.*

When you and your partners are both securely in your window of tolerance, choose a time to sit down and talk with them about your Hard Feelings. Take the time to discuss and identify what your different states of arousal look like, and the ways you can support each other during these times. Use the questions that follow to guide your conversation.

• How do you feel when you're in your window of tolerance?

• Can we talk about a time we handled a conversation that went really, really well?

• When you're upset, do you tend to get hyperaroused or hyporaroused? How can you tell?

• When you're out of your window of tolerance, what does that look like? How would I be able to tell?

- What are some things we can do to support each other when we have Hard Feelings?

- Can we talk about a time we had a conversation that went really, really wrong?

- How did that conversation get offtrack? Were we out of our windows?

- What's something you wish I would have done during that difficult conversation?

- What agreements can we make about appropriate behaviors during difficult conversations? What agreements can we make about handling our Hard Feelings?

- What are our strategies to soothe ourselves? What are our strategies to soothe each other?

- What kinds of resources do we need to better handle our Hard Feelings?

For Salomé and me, Hard Feelings became our new standard for navigating difficult conversations or uncomfortable moments. Rather than putting an emphasis on naming the specific shades and nuances of my emotions in the moment, or denying them to Salomé or myself, I was able to say, "I'm having some Hard Feelings. I don't know exactly what's going on, but it feels bad. I think I need some time to figure it out. Can you be patient with me while I think on this? I'm gonna write about it for a while. Then, once I feel more present, we can cuddle and talk a little, or maybe just watch a movie if I need more time."

Sometimes Salomé might say, "You seem really out of it. Is it Hard Feelings? I don't have the space to help you figure it out right now. Do you want some time to call a friend?"

This works so well for a few reasons. First, I can acknowledge that something is going on without feeling the pressure to solve it right then and there. This strategy also puts the onus on me to figure out my own state of mind and needs, rather than leave someone else guessing.

People are allowed to have emotional reactions. Assuming that someone will always be in their window of tolerance is unrealistic and unfair.

That's why we need strategies to deal with Hard Feelings before we have them. One of the most important ways to manage your Hard Feelings is to learn self-soothing strategies.

Self-Soothing

Self-soothing is anything you do to help regulate your emotional state. Self-soothing behaviors can return us to our window of tolerance. We calm down, move away from a state of arousal, and feel better.

Self-soothing is also valuable because it is something you do yourself. It's your own responsibility and your own power.

The behaviors you choose are up to you, and it can take some time to find the strategies that work for you. Following you'll find a few suggestions to get you started.

Measured Breathing. Count your breaths in and out, while trying to slow your heart rate.

Physical Activity. Go for a walk, blow off some steam with a run, or stretch to calm yourself down.

Distraction. Watch a movie, play your favorite album, or read a book. Try to get lost in something else for a while before returning to your emotions.

Reassurance. Keep a folder in your phone just of things that make you feel good and settled. Pictures of you and your loved ones. Screenshots of quotes, reminders, sweet text messages, and passages from your favorite books. Ask your partner to write you a note or letter with reassurances, and keep it in this album for when you need it. Anything that reminds you that you are loved, safe, and not alone in your Hard Feelings belongs in this folder.

Grounding. Take a cold shower. Drink something cold or hot. Wash your face or paint your nails. Try to focus on what you're doing in the moment, something repetitive and somatic.

Go through your self-soothing methods first. Then reach out for external support and help.

But if you struggle to self-soothe or find yourself grappling with chronic arousal that interferes with your well-being and quality of life, consider getting professional help. There are sex-positive and polyam therapists, counselors, and mental health professionals out there who want to help you. You don't have to do it alone.

Making Your Self-Soothing Plan

If you don't have a self-soothing plan, then now is the time to make one. Your plan can have as many steps as you need, and you're free to modify, repeat, and change your plan. Just don't be afraid to experiment! We all require different things at different times.

You can rely on this plan the next time you are out of your window of tolerance. It will be waiting for you before you even need it.

Step 1: *When I realize I'm out of my window of tolerance, the first thing I will do to self-soothe is:*

The reason I will do this first:

Step 2: *When I realize I'm out of my window of tolerance, the second thing I will do to self-soothe is:*

The reason I will do this second:

Step 3: *When I realize I'm out of my window of tolerance, the third thing I will do to self-soothe is:*

The reason I will do this third:

Self-soothing

SECTION 2

RULES, BOUNDARIES, AGREEMENTS, AND HOW WE CAN MAKE ROOM FOR POSITIVE CONFLICT

Section 1 was all about introducing you to the main themes of polyamory, with an emphasis on how you may begin to find the place, language, relationships, and desires that speak to you. Here, we'll be exploring the internal world: the desires, questions, fears, and curiosity that may leave us interested in, but perhaps intimidated by, polyamory.

Section 1 introduced the main organizing principles of this book, control and freedom. Section 2 is about the tools of the trade: how polyamory is actually *done*.

I often like to think of myself as a craftsperson. I want to build beautiful, stable, and functional structures. Relationships are just like houses or anything else I might build: they provide shelter, stability, warmth, and a place to meet and think and grow up. When the family expands and changes shape, so too must my house. As a craftsperson, the structures I build are my relationships and family.

But a craftsperson always needs good tools, the kind that are useful for and adaptable to a changing blueprint. In Section 2, I'm giving you the basics of building your own polyam structure: consent, conflict, boundaries, agreements, and apologies.

In Section 2, Chapter 5, I have a Q&A with author, speaker, and editor Crystal Byrd Farmer. I speak with Crystal about her work, her boundaries, and the undeniable messiness of being polyamorous. The questions she poses to herself and others come from more than a decade of trial and error, and reveal a wealth of knowledge about expectations, self-knowledge, and the logistics of polyam relationships. Crystal has *fourteen years* and counting of being polyamorous, and she's still navigating her boundaries, needs, and matching with partners who are truly compatible—showing us that the work of being polyam never really ends.

In Chapter 6, I introduce consent. This concept isn't just your responsibility to understand. It is your moral and ethical obligation to identify, use, and honor. Consent isn't only about sex either: that's just the tip of the iceberg. Consent will guide all aspects of how you deal with Hard Feelings and conflict, and how you hold yourself and others accountable.

Then, in Chapter 7, we get into the real bulk of this section by discussing rules, agreements, and boundaries. I go over these concepts carefully and compare them. Activities along the way help you really absorb their critical distinctions.

Finally, in Section 2, we bring all these ideas together as we talk about conflict and resolution. Conflict is unavoidable in relationships and in life. My hope is that the tools I offer in Section 2 will help you not only reframe how you think about or perhaps fear conflict, but also give you the means to resolve these conflicts in a healthy, secure manner.

In my estimation, Section 2 is the most complex of the book. I'm not just talking about the information. As you read through this section, you might find that uncomfortable emotions arise. You might remember past mistakes and feel shame or feel misunderstood. You might realize this section helps you put into words or better express a wrong done to you. You might feel anger or pain.

Take your time with this section—and with yourself. I invite you never to rush through these emotions or reactions. Write about them. Lean on the activities provided. Bring in a friend or partner to discuss what you're feeling. Use your tools. Craft the life you want.

Chapter 5

TALKING BOUNDARIES WITH CRYSTAL BYRD FARMER

I first came across Crystal—an author, an educator, and a speaker—through the website Black and Poly (www.blackandpoly.org), a community for Black people transitioning to polyamory. While reading through the site, I found Crystal's essay "The Triangle of Consent," which we'll use later in this book. As you read through our conversation, consider the questions Crystal asks of her potential partners and dates. Have you asked yourself these same questions yet?

SYG: Crystal, thanks so much for talking with me! Can you tell me a bit about yourself and the work you do?

CBF: I am Crystal Byrd Farmer (she/her), and I'm a writer and speaker. I was the editor of Black and Poly, a website for Black people and those who love them. I am in a lot of organizations and was an organizer for our local poly community. Right now, I'm on the board of the Foundation for Intentional Community, the copresident of the BIPOC Intentional Community Council, and a contributor and member of the editorial review board for *Communities* magazine.

My contributions to the poly world are giving workshops and writing about diversity. I also wrote "The Triangle of Consent," which is my safe sex communication model. My book *The Token* was published in 2020 and is a guidebook for communities that want to increase their diversity. I describe the experiences many marginalized people face and have discussion questions for leaders to work through while doing "the work." I have several examples from the poly and sex-positive communities in the book as well.

I cofounded an Agile Learning Center called Gastonia Freedom School. This center supports disabled children with self-directed learning. I have been on several podcasts and interviews, and I definitely don't remember them all [they include *Panel: Decentering Whiteness in Consensual Nonmonogamy*, *Multiamory*, *How We Talk About Sex* with Eric Leviton, and *Sisters of Sexuality* with Taylor Sparks]. Some are listed on my website, www.crystalbyrdfarmer.com. I live in Gastonia, North Carolina, and I have one child.

SYG: Thanks, Crystal. Now for a barrage of questions! Tell me about your nonmonogamous journey. How long have you been nonmonogamous, and what drew you to nonmonogamy? What was your learning curve like? What did you read, listen to, or talk about to help that learning curve?

CBF: I have been nonmonogamous for fourteen years. I started off by having lots of sex with people from Craigslist, then I joined the local BDSM [bondage, dominance, submission, and masochism] community, then I got married, then I got divorced, and now I'm solo poly. I like to tell people that I have all the horror stories.

I started with Craigslist because I was just out of college and in a new city. I had only one boyfriend in college and was pretty conservative sexually. I was interested in exploring my sexuality, and I didn't know anyone in town. I identify as bi but I was interested in all kinds of sex with all kinds of people. I quickly discovered that I was a slut and that sex was a special interest for me (I'm autistic). I loved the whole process of talking to people, establishing our shared interests, fucking, and the going away.

I considered myself during that time to be "unethically monogamous" because while I knew how to take care of myself physically, I wasn't taking care of my emotions or the emotions of others. I got involved with the local BDSM community, and that's where I learned more about ethics, boundaries, and communication. I'm sure I read the books, but I don't remember any of their advice sticking because I'm pretty stubborn. I had to get hurt a lot to realize I wanted to do things differently.

Back then, it was basically *The Ethical Slut* by Dossie Easton and Janet Hardy and maybe *Opening Up* by Tristan Taormino. I was around when *More Than Two* by Franklin Veaux and Eve Rickert was published, and it was a big deal.

But the learning curve was slow and full of pain. I used to do Poly 101s in Charlotte, and I realize that you really can't tell people and expect them to listen. Most of them have to see it for themselves.

SYG: I'd like to talk about boundaries. What does a boundary mean to you? How do you communicate those boundaries—and respect others' boundaries? What are some of the most important boundaries you have?

CBF: In my relationships, I can only control myself. I do not tell my partners what to do, and I don't even know what they're doing with other people half the time—most of the time. I start with my boundaries at the very beginning of talking to people, even before we meet in person, because even now I'm the type to have sex on the first date. Here are some of my boundaries.

No kissing. I've been trying to figure out the reason for this since I read *Polysecure* last year but it's still a mystery. It triggers a lot of emotions for me, and I generally don't like having emotions (again, I'm autistic). Sex requires a lot of vulnerability, but maybe kissing requires more. When I talk to my partners about romantic intimacy, I feel a lot of stress and sadness. So I'm still figuring that out.

I will tell new partners my test results and that one of my partners has HSV [herpes simplex virus], an STI. I trust my partners to keep me updated on their results, but I don't ask to see papers or anything. In all my years of sluttiness, I've only had HPV [human papillomavirus] and trich [trichomoniasis]. My mantra is, "If you don't trust them, you shouldn't be fucking them."

I don't give emotional support. You might need to add a whole section about how autism works in polyamory. I generally don't feel emotions, and it is a lot of work for me to give emotional support to other people. So I generally don't. My partners know this. If they want it from me, they know they have to say what they need, because all I know to say is, "Poor baby." Or have sex with them. It works for me.

After reading *Polysecure* I wondered if this was a good boundary, and I played around with talking about my emotions more with my partners. It sucked. I used to be codependent, so having emotions apparently triggers me and makes me feel anxious and depressed. I terrorized one of my partners for several weeks trying to explain how these emotions showed up whenever he did or didn't do something. For instance, I told him I was excited when we planned a date, but when he canceled I told him I was sad and how that connected to past trauma and stuff. I hated it. I love being in a neutral emotional state and not putting any expectations on my partners in terms of what we will or will not do. I know if they want to be with me, they will get in touch. I have never been able to see or hear subtext in conversations, so I take everything my partners say at face value. They know I will be completely honest with them.

SYG: How do you vet potential partners: Is it a conversation, a gut feeling, a case-by-case basis? How do you find out if your values are compatible with a potential partner? What does that conversation look like?

CBF: I am an incessant and intrusive questioner. One of my longest-term partners told me it was "too much" at the beginning, but I'm okay with that. Here are some of my questions:

- How long have you been poly?

- What do your current relationships look like?

- What are your relationship agreements?

- What is your sexual health plan?

- Do you have a history of codependency?

- How do you deal with jealousy?

- Is sex at your house possible, or do you have rules around that? (I don't usually have sex at my house.)

- What do your children know about your relationships? (I think it's important to be honest in an age-appropriate way with children.)

- Are you involved in the local poly community?

- Do you practice hierarchy?

- Are you kinky?

- Why did your most recent relationship end?

- What kind of sex do you like?

- How often do you see your partners?

- (If they're a couple) Whose idea was it to explore poly?

- Why did your last relationship end?

SYG: Do you have agreements in your relationships around communication, finances, living situations, specific boundaries, etc.? Why do those agreements matter? How did you negotiate them?

CBF: I love my triangle of consent model, because for me it incorporates things that are important to me, like agency. I don't pick up on subtext, so I need people to be clear and up-front with me. Otherwise, I will be in the dark because I don't make the same assumptions about relationships that other people make. Here are some of my agreements (actually, they are statements). If the other person is not okay with them, then we're not a match.

- I will let you know if my test results change. I don't need to see your papers: just let me know if there is something new.

- I only do kink with experienced kinky people.

- I will let you know when I want to see you, and you should do the same. I don't do small talk or "good night" texts. I will send memes to my favorite people, but you have to tell me if that's something you want.

- I have two people I do emotional support stuff with. I will reach out to them when I need it. I generally won't be able to do emotional support with you, meaning, don't text me when you're sad because you won't get much sympathy. If you want to come over and cry, you're going to have to call someone else.

- We don't share finances. You can buy me dinner or pay for a date. I don't make much money, so don't expect us to do extravagant events or travel unless you're paying.

- I have a child. Sometimes I have to cancel to take care of her. Very often, I won't have someone to watch her. I generally only go out once a week, not including all the meetings and organizations I'm a part of. That means you're a part of a cycle of three or four people that I make time for. I've actually been trying to do more with my partners besides going to their house and having sex, but it means that my daughter is coming along with us. Most of my partners are okay with that. She is autistic though and very sensory defensive. That means we're not doing any loud restaurants, nothing that requires sitting for a long time, and nothing that is "adults only." It's just an additional dynamic.

- My daughter only has two parents. I'm happy for my partners to interact with her like I described above, but they are not there to take care of her. Many of my partners buy her gifts for Christmas or her birthday. But discipline is a no. Helping her self-regulate is a no. "Teaching" her anything is a no (we're unschoolers).

- I'm not going to move in, but I will spend the night if I have a babysitter or if my daughter can too. After I left my husband, I moved into my dad's house, which he doesn't live in, but he was uncomfortable with me having partners over. So for years I was just meeting up at my partners' houses. They come over now but it's still lopsided. So they have to be willing to "host." It's similar with traveling or any kind of adventure they want to take me on. They'll have to pay most of the cost, and they can expect my daughter to be there if it's more than a full day. So, needless to say, this doesn't happen very often.

- I'll tell you if something in my life changes that affects us being together. I get new relationship energy (NRE)[2] really hard, so I make sure to tell new people that at some point I won't be as obsessed over them. I expect the same, but in my experience they are not as aware of how their feelings change over time.

----

2   New relationship energy, or NRE, describes the excitement and state of mind people often experience in the early stages of a new relationship. These feelings are usually intense sexual attraction and infatuation, which some people describe as feeling high or lovesick—and it's totally normal! Usually, these feelings fade in time, and the relationship becomes a deeper, but more stable, companionship. In nonmonogamy, NRE can be especially tricky because there are multiple relationships to balance and maintain.

SYG: How does it feel in your body when you are respected, cherished, and supported in your relationships? What does that look like? What does a "successful" polycule look like for you and your loved ones?

CBF: Blame the autism—because I have no idea. It's very difficult to associate my body feelings with what's going on outside me. My successful relationships are full of communication, realistic expectations, and good sex. When I notice myself feeling uncomfortable or anxious about seeing someone, that's a sign that something is off. So I "downshift" those relationships.

SYG: Later on in this book, I'll be talking about accountability: how to acknowledge harm, hold space for others, make amends, and change behavior. Can you talk about a time when you needed accountability from someone? What happened, what did it look like, how was it addressed?

CBF: I wrote a piece on Medium about Reid Mihalko, and I was also part of Eve Rickert's accountability pod for Franklin Veaux. What a mess! In my black-and-white world, accountability is really easy. If I'm wrong or I caused harm, I apologize. Normal people don't do it well. They get very defensive and take things personally. They resist changing their behavior. They use their social clout to get out of real accountability. All of that is frustrating to me.

I was part of a community called New Culture, and I experienced some harm over three years at their summer camp. I didn't handle it well, but they also didn't handle it well. It took several years for me to be able to articulate the harm, and by then I was able to dialogue about it with some of them. It was really great, and I feel like we have good relationships now.

What happened: New Culture Summer Camp East is "sex camp" for hippie-dippie people. They have never had a lot of diversity, and I was the only Black person there the first summer I went. I experienced a lot of discomfort even though I loved being there. Part of it was my difficulty engaging with the mindfulness/bodywork aspects of the camp because, as I've said, I'm autistic. Part of it was hating being in a camp environment with no creature comforts. The food was mostly vegan, and I simply can't eat certain things. Despite all that, I went back two more years.

The second year they asked me to help present about diversity, which was a mistake. Since then I've become an official "diversity consultant," and I set better boundaries about how I engage in that labor. I got the brunt end of a lot of negative comments, and there was also a kerfuffle about the trans people who were there. It was very demoralizing. The third year, I got food poisoning and stayed in bed most of the week. So after that I was very critical about the way they did things. I'm still critical but I am able to talk to them about it without negativity. There's also some more info on accountability and representation on my website and the Black and Poly site too.

SYG: In this book, I talk a lot about control and freedom, and how those two forces inform our relationships. What is your personal definition of freedom? What does a free relationship look like to you? How does it feel? When do you know you're in a relationship that prioritizes freedom?

CBF: Freedom is the ability to move through my life without other people complaining. Or they should at least keep it to themselves. I recognize that I'm a difficult person to be in a relationship with, so I want my partners to take care of themselves. If something's not working, they should change it—no matter how it affects me. Same for my life.

I sometimes experience a desire to get out of my box and extend myself for my people. I wouldn't say it's not rewarded, but it just doesn't feel like it's worth the effort. I learned in Al-Anon that expectations are future disappointments. If I am not being realistic, then things are not going to feel good. So I know I'm experiencing freedom when I don't feel like I am getting a lot of requests to go out of my comfort zone, and when I feel comfortable enough to tell my people when I need to adjust.

Chapter 6

CONSENT

Consent is something everyone, not just nonmonogamous folks, must understand and bring into their relationships. Often we assume that consent applies only to the realm of sex or physical contact. In reality, consent should inform everything we do.

In the glossary near the beginning of this book, I define *consent*. Take a moment to reread that definition here:

Consent is a voluntary, fully informed, and risk aware agreement. These three pieces of consent are very important, so I'll break them down. Consent must be voluntary, meaning no one is under pressure or duress to make any particular decision; to be voluntary means each person *genuinely* wants something to happen, be it sex or a relationship, and there are no consequences if they do *not* want it to happen. Consent should be fully informed, meaning everyone has all the information, knowledge, and context needed to make a voluntary decision.

And finally, consent should be risk aware, meaning someone is fully informed of potential risks and is able to decide what is best for them. For example, imagine you are going to have sex with someone, and they inform you that they've had unprotected sex recently. They also inform you that it's been three years since their most recent STI (sexually transmitted infection) test. You now have a better understanding of the potential risk that comes along with having sex with this person. You may decide to mitigate that risk with safer sex precautions or barrier methods, or you may decide to not have sex. Either way, you were risk aware and therefore better able to provide or decline consent.

To deepen this conversation, I'm drawing from Crystal Byrd Farmer's triangle of consent model. Although she discusses this model mainly in the sexual sense, I believe it can, and should, be applied more broadly. Take a look at the model, which follows.

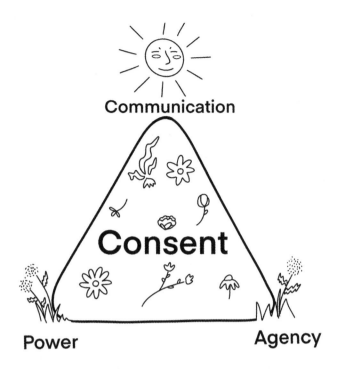

Crystal writes that the triangle of consent "starts with the recognition of agency and power balances and ends with specific communication about sexual acts. This model has the form of a triangle in equal relationship to each other. If one part is missing or abbreviated, it will affect the entire experience of giving and obtaining consent. Here are the three legs: agency, power, and communication."

Agency

Agency, or what I would call freedom, is the first leg of the triangle. Crystal defines agency as the "recognition that we all have the ability to make choices for ourselves."

The choices we make should be fully informed and risk aware. This means that if someone *should* know something to make a decision for themselves, they need to have that information. For example, if you go on a date with someone new, then they should be aware you are nonmonogamous. That information will affect their ability to decide whether you are a good match. You should also be forthcoming about your level of experience with nonmonogamy for the same reasons.

But, as Crystal points out, we also need to be aware of cognition or "each person's ability to understand the situation."

Drugs, drinking, age, disability status, mental condition, and emotional state all influence a person's agency. Be aware and abundantly cautious when it comes to giving relevant information and gauging cognition. The less you know someone, the less you should make assumptions about what information they need, their ability to fully understand it, and their capacity to make choices for themselves.

Power

The next leg of the triangle is power. Crystal writes that "any relationship between two people is subject to a power imbalance when someone has more seniority, wealth, status, or social support than their partner....The power dynamics of each relationship is not fixed, and it's always subjective. If someone believes they have less power, that will impact their ability to give consent."

Following is a list of things that give power to someone *over* another societally and culturally. This power can and often does bleed into the interpersonal sphere. This list is by no means exhaustive, but use it as a conversation starter:

- Racial privilege
- Class privilege and wealth
- Gender privilege, including cis-ness
- Seniority or experience
- Familial support
- Heterosexuality
- Citizenship

- Physical ability/lack of disability

- Neurotypical

Next, think about the ways your power may affect your consent practices:

- Do you make visible the power you hold?

- How do you acknowledge and mitigate the power you have?

- Have you ever used your power to get what you want? How?

- How do you react when someone tells you no?

- If someone says no, then would they fear consequences from you?

- When was the most recent time you talked about power in your relationships?

If you are in a relationship with power imbalances (most of us are), then you need to think of the ways you can better create a safe environment for your partner to truly express their desires and what they wholeheartedly consent to. The best way to do this? Educate yourself on the identities and power you hold. A great place to start is the recommended reading list in the back of this book. While in the process of educating yourself, you can also ask your loved ones how you can do better. Take their word for it.

If you are the person with less power in the relationship, remember it's not your responsibility to teach your partner how to treat you with respect or understand your background or identity. Likewise, it's not your job to hold your partner's hand through their own growth at the expense of your well-being or safety. If someone treats you poorly and uses their power to avoid accountability or self-edification, you have every right to exit that relationship or interaction. Remember, mistakes are inevitable—it's the reaction that matters.

Communication

The last leg of the triangle is communication. Communication requires truth and the willingness to give details and offer vulnerability.

To achieve agency, acknowledge power, and reach consent, *you have to talk about it!* But communication does not always need to be verbal.

If you're having a conversation with your boyfriend about canceled plans and it starts to get overwhelming, then switch to passing notes back and forth. Use agreed-upon safe words, such as "Break out," as a shorthand to communicate that you need a break or alone time. A favorite nonverbal consent marker for me and my partners is the "double tap." If anyone is at all uncomfortable, then we tap twice on the other person to let them know it's time to stop or change something.

The important thing with nonverbal communication markers is that they're discussed *ahead* of an intense conversation, social situation, or sex. But other than that, you and your partners are allowed to decide what communication looks like for you.

Together, agency, power, and communication create a space in which consent can thrive.

Chapter 7

THE THREE DYNAMICS: RULES, AGREEMENTS, AND BOUNDARIES

In my experience, rules, agreements, and boundaries are the three main ways relationships are managed. These three dynamics do not apply to every relationship in the same way. In an ideal world, rules, agreements, and boundaries are always distinct, separate, and tidy. In reality, they can overlap. They can get messy or bleed into one another, and it can become difficult to judge what's fair and realistic, as opposed to what's controlling. What I offer here are estimations to help guide you and figure out what you do and do not want.

You should always ask others to clarify what exactly they mean when they say certain words and refer to certain dynamics, because my definitions are not universal. Remember what I said about assumptions in Chapter 2 on page 37? (Don't assume others understand you. Instead, do the hard work of communicating.) It always applies.

What I share here are tools to describe and identify what you do want and what you don't want. These tools, as always, are based on my goal of attaining personal and relational freedom from any attempt to unfairly restrict myself or others. My nonmonogamous practice prioritizes agency, and I'll do my best to make my personal opinions visible throughout this section.

As you read, think about how agency, power, and communication—the three corners of consent—do or do not factor into each dynamic.

Rules

A rule is anything that dictates the behavior of someone else. For this conversation, we're defining rules as an external force—we put rules on others or they put rules on us. Rules have a few key characteristics:

- Rules are decided based on unrealistic expectations.

- Rules are laid down for you by someone else (or vice versa); you don't have a say in them.

- If you break a rule, then there are consequences.

- Rules are made in response to or in anticipation of uncomfortable emotions or fears.

- Rules try to avoid discomfort and conflict—but end up causing both.

- Rules come from a scarcity mindset.

- Rules are often a controlling reaction to the normal but uncomfortable realities of being nonmonogamous.

- Rules make your emotions other people's problems and vice versa.

- Rules often coddle your discomfort rather than allowing you to grow past it.

- Rules often require surveillance of someone's else behavior and choices.

- Rules undermine agency.

Example: Joanna and her partner, Leon, are considering going nonmonogamous. They decide to set some ground rules, with the intention of keeping their core relationship secure and unthreatened by anyone else. Joanna feels uncomfortable with Leon dating someone she doesn't like. But really, she's also nervous that Leon will meet someone cooler and more attractive than she is, especially because she's not seeing anyone right now or particularly thrilled with her dating options.

Joanna and Leon decide to have a veto rule, meaning if Joanna doesn't like someone Leon wants to sleep with, then she can veto that person. The same applies to Joanna if Leon doesn't like her potential lover. They decide that a veto is a no-questions-asked rule: once the veto is invoked, contact must be cut off immediately.

Why it doesn't work: This kind of rule doesn't work because it's not up to Joanna or Leon who their partners see and love. This rule is controlling and prioritizes one person's insecurities over another's freedom. You don't have to *like* your metamour, but you do have the responsibility to deal with your own insecurities and respect your partner's decisions. In this scenario, the veto will lead to resentment and conflict between Joanna, Leon, and their future metamours (who, by the way, get no say in this at *all*).

Why I hate it: Rules are based on control. They come at the cost of someone else's agency and power. If your partner decides to continue seeing someone you vetoed, then they will face unfair consequences from you and communication breakdowns will follow. Look back at the triangle of consent: this rule affects every leg of consent, as most do. To me, rules are deeply unethical.

RULES ACTIVITY

Think about the rules that have been imposed on you throughout your life, even as a child. Rules can be as simple as "You have to finish your plate before you leave the table" or as complex as "Never go to bed angry."

But what if you had a big lunch and just aren't hungry? Now, apparently, you have to force-feed yourself.

Or what if you need extra time to get back into your window of tolerance? You have good reason to be angry, and you aren't ready to talk. Why force it? You'd just get into an even bigger argument!

Neither of these rules is contextual or responsive to your needs. Take a few moments to fill out the following chart of rules you were told to follow and the results of those rules. The chart begins with an example.

Rule	Consequence
You need to be back from an overnight date by 8 a.m. so I can see you before I leave for work.	My ability to decide what to do with my day and how to spend my time were negatively affected. I missed out on having a great breakfast with someone I really care about. I feel resentful.

Agreements

Agreements are negotiated commitments between partners. Agreements spell out shared expectations for behavior. Here are their characteristics:

- Agreements are flexible, contextual, and frequently revisited and updated.

- Agreements are fully understood and fully informed.

- Agreements offer models for what behavior should look like around conflict, Hard Feelings, sex, and communication.

- Agreements are realistic and ethical protocol for a relationship.

- Agreements are meant to help you grow and mature.

- Agreements reject ultimatums.

- Agreements are not punishment.

- Agreements are based in agency.

Example: Maeve and their partner, Jas, are new to nonmonogamy. Jas has been on a few different dating apps and decided she wants to ask out a cute girl she's been chatting with for a few days, Leah. Maeve checks out Leah's profile. Leah is beautiful and fascinating, a freelance photographer who travels frequently and has the kind of artistic, sophisticated vibe Maeve's always wanted. Maeve realizes she feels insecure and a little threatened by Leah.

A day before the date, Maeve and Jas sit down to check in. Maeve tells Jas that she's feeling a little possessive and worried, but that she doesn't want her feelings to put a damper on something so exciting and new. Jas reassures her, and they both decide to have some sort of protocol for dealing with dates.

They discuss the situation for a while and agree that during dates, Maeve and Jas won't text or otherwise communicate. They also agree that time on dates with other lovers should be free of distractions unless there is an emergency. In addition, they agree that they both need time to acclimate to the discomfort and adrenaline that will arise from seeing new people. Maeve tells Jas that she'd like to hear about the date as soon as she gets home because her imagination often runs wild, but Jas objects. She wants time to decompress and process after a date—not feel like she has to report back and answer a ton of questions she's not ready for. They talk for a while and find a realistic solution: when someone gets home from a date, they'll take a few hours to wind down. Then either Maeve or Jas will ask for consent before discussing the date. They also agree that if someone feels activated by Hard Feelings, the first course of action is to self-soothe rather than immediately unload on the other person.

Maeve and Jas reassure each other that this agreement isn't set in stone, and as they both go on more dates, they will revisit this conversation when they find out what aspects of the agreement either work or don't work.

Why it works: This agreement works because it's realistic and flexible. Both partners are assuming the best intentions of the other and working together to agree on expected behaviors. Maeve acknowledges her insecurity and jealousy, but doesn't make Jas responsible for dealing with it. Meanwhile, Jas feels she can enjoy her dates without worrying about calming Maeve down. Her need for processing time is also met. Both partners have realistic expectations about what will happen during and after a date.

Why I love it: Agreements are the healthy version of a rule: communication is happening but rather than leveraging power to force behavior and avoid normal discomfort, Maeve and Jas are working together to support one another while still honoring their mutual commitment to freedom and agency.

Unlike the veto rule example, both partners are expressing their needs and feelings without jeopardizing the other's agency or power. Maeve isn't using her insecurity to manipulate Jas's choice in dates. Jas isn't telling Maeve to get over her feelings. Instead, Maeve and Jas are using agreements to maintain their connection and work through new experiences as a team. You'll also notice that the three legs of consent are maintained and respected in this scenario.

AGREEMENTS ACTIVITY

Agreements can be very challenging to reach. Sometimes we may even put off important conversations out of fear that they won't go well.

Think about some of the issues you and your partners may be avoiding. How can agreements support communication? How can you reframe these issues as something to connect on and negotiate through?

An issue I've been meaning to talk about:

Something I've noticed:

I think we need to revisit:

Boundaries

A boundary is something that dictates *your* behavior in a certain situation or context. Boundaries also clarify your expectations around personal behavior, physical space, personal possessions, privacy, sex, time, and beliefs.

- Boundaries are about your individual needs.

- Boundaries are not up for debate or negotiation.

- Boundaries are realistic, responsive, and responsible.

- Boundaries are never used as punishment.

- Boundaries can be rigid, permeable, or flexible—but that's up to you.

- Boundaries are different from agreements because they are something having to do with only your own behavior and needs.

- Boundaries aren't rules because they do not dictate another person's behavior. Rather, they respond to it.

Following are a few examples of boundaries because there can be a lot of confusion about what a boundary looks or sounds like.

Examples

If you yell at me, then I'm leaving the room. (Personal behavior)

Don't touch my wheelchair or try to push me unless I let you know that I need help. (Physical space)

Don't borrow my clothes without asking. (Personal possessions)

I keep my phone and computer password protected so only I have access to them. (Privacy)

I don't give oral sex. (Sex)

I like to have my quiet time after 9:00 p.m. I don't answer texts after that time, but if it's an emergency you can call me. (Time)

My religion isn't up for debate. If you continue to question my beliefs, then I will leave. (Beliefs)

Why we need them: Boundaries are ways we can protect our time, energy, mental well-being, and physical safety. Boundaries prioritize our needs and agency, based on what we do and do not consent to be around or be exposed to.

Why I love them: Boundaries exist apart from agreements or rules. They're about *you* and what you need.

How to accept them: It can be emotionally challenging to hear someone else's boundary. It can feel like rejection or a personal affront. But the more you practice accepting another's boundary, the easier it becomes. A few tips for accepting boundaries follow.

- Thank them for sharing.

- Be curious and ask clarifying questions.

- Keep a little note in your phone or journal of your partner's boundaries. It will help you remember them!

- Don't judge someone else's needs.

- Don't test the boundary.

- Don't claim ignorance of the boundary once it's been stated.

- Ask yourself, Am I centering myself and my feelings rather than someone else's realistic needs? Why?

BOUNDARIES ACTIVITY

Take a moment to think about the boundaries you have around personal behavior, physical space, personal possessions, privacy, sex, time, and beliefs.

When was the most recent time you expressed them? Revisited them? Let's do that now together.

Physical Space	

The Polyamory Workbook

Personal Possessions	
Personal Behavior	
Privacy	
Sex	
Time	
Beliefs	

Putting It All Together

Take a look at the chart that follows. You'll find three columns, labeled variously " Rule," "Agreement," and " Boundary." Read each situation provided, and then reframe it to correspond to a rule, an agreement, and a boundary.

To get you started, the first three rows have been completed for you.

As you fill out the chart, look back to the triangle of consent model. Ask yourself, What happens to agency, power, and communication as each scenario moves from rule to agreement to boundary?

Rule	Agreement	Boundary
You're not allowed to have unprotected sex with anyone but me.	We agree to have protected sex with one-night stands. Protected sex looks like using condoms and dental dams, no fluid swapping, cleaning toys before and after each use, and _____.	If you have unprotected sex with someone, then I won't have sex with you until you get an STI test.
You're not allowed to see your ex because it makes me uncomfortable.	We agree that when partner A hangs out with their ex, partner B will not be available for emotional support before or after the hangout. We agree to talk about partner A's ex under the circumstances that _____.	If you hang out with your ex, then I don't want to hear the details.
You have to break up with your polyam partners and be monogamous with me.	We agree to be in a monogamous relationship. This means we have agreed not to have sex or erotic romance outside this relationship. This looks like _____.	I don't date polyamorous people.
	We agree not to raise our voices during conflict. If someone starts to yell, then they will get one reminder. If they continue to yell after that reminder, then the other person will leave the room or house. We agree that an apology is needed after all parties have cooled off.	

The Polyamory Workbook

Rule	Agreement	Boundary
I'm allowed to read your texts and dating app messages.		
You're allowed to have sex with other women only if I'm watching.		I have sex with other consenting adults on my own terms.
	We agree to use our best discretion when it comes to informing families, friends, and coworkers that we all live together as partners. This looks like _____.	

Rule	Agreement	Boundary

The Polyamory Workbook

Conflict

Conflict is hard to define. I struggle to put such a far-reaching and deeply impactful concept such as *conflict* into simple terms. We know what conflict can feel like: a gap, a tension, a *Why don't you agree with what I'm saying?* Sometimes conflict can feel like an explosion waiting to happen. Other times, it can feel like a release of pressure and the start of true connection.

For my definition, I turn to Sarah Schulman's 2016 book *Conflict Is Not Abuse: Overstating Harm, Community Responsibility, and the Duty of Repair.* Schulman, a lesbian activist, a writer, a professor, and an AIDS historian, writes that conflict is "rooted in difference and people are and always will be different."

Difference is the human condition: difference of opinion, culture, language, gender, ability, ethnicity, race, experience, and values. The list goes on and on. But difference is not wrongness.

Conflict gets out of hand when difference becomes, *You are wrong. I am right.* Rather, conflict should be, *I understand you and you understand me. Let's work toward a compromise.*

Now, of course, we need to use reason and context when assessing conflict, difference, and wrongness. A difference in world view can also mean unchecked assumptions of power and an entitlement to oppress and hurt others: racists, incels, and fascists have a different world view than I do. I'm confident in saying they are wrong. I'm fine saying, I am in conflict—irreparable conflict—with these differences.

But there's a *very* important distinction between conflict that escalates to, *You are wrong. I am right,* and conflict that escalates to, *You are wrong and therefore less than me. I am right and therefore more than you.*

In this book, I'm talking about the former kind of conflict, the kind that arises from reasonable difference. This kind of *reasonable* conflict often leads to a fight, or argument, about shared values, acceptable behaviors, or mistaken understanding.

Fights happen when difference leads us to disconnect from empathy, critical thinking, personal reflection, or change.

But if you learn to avoid fighting and embrace difference, reasonable conflict can actually be an opportunity for positive change, learning, and growth in relationships.

Reframing Conflict

Conflict is an opportunity to explore difference. It may look like an intense conversation, a series of conversations, or phone calls with physical distance, but the mark of *healthy* conflict is that you and your loved one are able to maintain empathy, critical thinking, personal reflection, and openness to change.

While in conflict, you have the chance to examine your unchecked assumptions, integrate another person's opinions and experiences into your own world view, change your mind, own up to your mistakes, or find common ground. In this way, conflict can actually bring you and your loved one closer together.

- Conflict is an opportunity to better understand your partner and how they think.

- Conflict is an opportunity to better understand how *you* think.

- Conflict can be affirming: your loved one cares enough about the relationship to risk disconnection in the hope of being heard and respected.

- Conflict can be empowering: you feel secure enough in your relationship with a loved one to tell them when something needs to be addressed.

- Conflict can lead to a mutual understanding and a respect of difference—without pointing fingers or keeping score of who's right or wrong.

- Conflict can force you to release pride, let down your defenses, and be vulnerable.

- Conflict requires you to be creative in reaching solutions to a problem.

- Conflict can lead to a stronger relationship.

- Conflict can lead to compromise and agreements on future behaviors.

- Conflict can lead to the creation of boundaries.

- Conflict is a space in which you can communicate effectively.

- Conflict is a space in which you can realize you've made a mistake.

- Conflict can expose your blind spots, assumptions, and unfair behaviors.

- Conflict can be a positive space in which you and your loved ones learn to work together, make good on promises, and live out your ideals.

- Conflict is often a precursor to accountability.

ACTIVITY: REFRAMING YOUR CONFLICTS

Take a moment to reflect on the kind of conflict you've had in the past or are navigating presently.

Do these conflicts usually follow a pattern of difference, escalation, and fighting?

At what point does a conflict escalate into a fight? What do you do: get defensive, make accusations, cry, shut down, or raise your voice? How do you wish you could act instead?

Are there any themes that cause the fights you have? Jealousy? Dirty dishes and household labor? Last-minute cancellations? Money and bills?

How can you use agreements, boundaries, and the triangle of consent to help resolve conflict?

What's your plan to reframe conflict? How do you want to handle conflict in the future and prevent fights? How will you talk to your partners about this? How will you make healthy conflict the standard in your life?

Accountability

Conflict often starts or ends with the need for accountability. At its core, *accountability* means taking responsibility for your actions and making amends.

Taking accountability for your actions has three main steps.

1. Acknowledgment of your actions and their impact on others

Acknowledgment starts with truly understanding and absorbing what another person says to you. Allow the injured party to express their emotions, and resist the urge to make excuses, interject, or get defensive. The point here isn't to argue your case or take attention away from the injured party: it's to actively listen and understand their point of view.

Here are a few ways to affirm and clarify your understanding.

- I've been listening to what you're saying, and I want to make sure I understand you clearly. Can I restate what you've told me to make sure I've got it right?

- I'm trying to listen and understand, but I'm not sure what you meant when you said _____. I think that meant something like _____, but I don't want to assume. Can you clarify, so we're on the same page?

- I'm trying to keep up with everything you're saying, but I'm getting a little overwhelmed. I'm going to write down some things as you're talking and then once you're done speaking, I'd like to read back what I got. I'm doing this to make sure I stay present and process what you're saying. How does that sound?

After the injured party has said their piece, ask if it's a good time for you to acknowledge your errors and their impact. Acknowledge what happened: the situation, your actions, and how what you did affected the injured party. Speak bluntly about your actions.

Often, naming *exactly* what you did wrong is the hardest part of being accountable. Sometimes you might want to skip right to an apology, rather than admit what happened. Resist this urge. Instead, own up to what you did. It lets your loved one know that you understand what role you played in what happened, and that you can communicate this despite experiencing difficult emotions, including shame.

- Is this a good time for me to talk about my role in this situation? I'd like to acknowledge what I've done and how it hurt you: _____.

- I did [insert action here] last night and crossed [insert boundary here] by doing [insert details here]. When I did this, you felt [insert emotion here]. Then I escalated the situation by [insert action here].

2. An apology

An apology isn't just saying, "I'm sorry," and it's definitely not skirting accountability with the classic, "I'm sorry you *feel* that way." A quality apology requires empathy and remorse. Let's discuss these.

Empathy is the ability to relate to and feel the experiences of another. You put yourself in someone else's shoes. Empathy sounds like, *How would I feel if I were treated this way?*

Remorse is regret for what you did. Remorse can feel like a mix of guilt and wanting to "take back" what you did. It requires *understanding* why your actions were not appropriate and the hurt your actions caused. Remorse sounds like, *I regret what I did because I understand its impact. I need to fix this.*

A good apology might sound like this:

- I'm sorry that I treated you that way. I regret what I did, and you have every right to be feeling the way you do.

- I really apologize for my actions. I wish I had never done that. You didn't deserve to be treated that way.

- I'm sorry for what I did yesterday. My actions were irresponsible, hurtful, and unacceptable. I should never have said those things. I can't undo what I did, but I am committed to making this right.

3. Amends

Amends are your plans for future behavior. They show that your apology meant something. Amends are the embodiment of "walk the talk" and a chance to realign your values with your actions.

This plan is the responsibility of the party at fault. Sometimes the injured party will want to help make a plan to prevent the error from happening again, but their participation should never be assumed.

The start of a good plan might sound like this:

* I have a few ideas on how to prevent my mistake from happening again. The first thing I will do is _____.

* Now that we've talked this through and I've had some time to think, I'm realizing I need more support in this area. I plan to book an appointment with my therapist to talk about better coping strategies. I also plan to go back to my support group.

* In the future, I'm going to rely more on my self-soothing strategies before sharing my feelings with you. The next time I feel angry, I'm going to take a break and go for a run before trying to talk. I also spoke with my friend, who said I could reach out to them if I need to vent. I'm planning on reading a new book on managing stress and bringing what I learn into my life.

Let's put everything together. An example of a really good apology follows.

Example: Meaningful Accountability

Situation: Malcolm and Oliver are polyamorous and share a two-bedroom apartment. Malcolm and Oliver have separate rooms. Each partner uses his own room to have sleepovers and dates, and it's been working well. The men made an agreement about dates: when the door is closed, it means privacy is needed. If a date is not present, then the other partner may knock and ask to enter. If a date is being hosted and the door is closed, then this means do not disturb or knock unless there is an emergency. Both Malcolm and Oliver feel this arrangement is very fair and realistic, but it's especially important to Malcolm, who really values privacy.

The previous night, however, Oliver heard Malcolm and his date, Dre, laughing and having sex in Malcolm's room. Malcolm's door was closed. Oliver tried to ignore the noises at first, but he let his jealousy get the better of him. He stormed into Malcolm's room and told them to keep it down. Oliver could tell that Malcolm and Dre were shocked and embarrassed. Shortly after, Malcolm and Dre left the apartment together. Malcolm texted Oliver not to expect him back for a couple of days. He would be staying at Dre's apartment, and Oliver was to refrain from speaking to Malcolm until he got home.

Two days later, Malcolm comes home and says he needs to talk about the other night. The two sit down together. Malcolm cries and says he's still really upset, confused, and angered by Oliver's actions. His privacy was violated. And he feels humiliated that Oliver saw him and Dre in the middle of sex.

Dre, whom Malcolm has been seeing on and off for five years, was also extremely uncomfortable and told Malcolm he didn't want to sleep over at his apartment anymore. Malcolm tells Oliver that his actions affect not only Malcolm and Oliver's relationship, but also Malcolm's relationship with Dre, someone he loves and cares about. Malcolm tells Oliver that he gets jealous sometimes too when Oliver has dates, but he would never try to humiliate him in front of anyone, ever.

After listening to Malcolm and reflecting on his behavior for the past couple of days, Oliver understands that he needs to be accountable for his actions.

Oliver: I'm so sorry for the pain I've caused you. Do you need to vent more or are you open to me apologizing?

Malcolm: I've said everything I can say right now. But I need you to hear how angry I am.

Oliver: I do hear it. The other night, I was so immature. I knew ahead of time that you would have Dre over, but I didn't prepare myself well enough, mentally or emotionally. I heard you guys having fun and having sex and instead of dealing with my own jealousy, I took it out on you. I violated our agreement about closed doors. I knew what I was doing wasn't okay, but I did it anyway. I violated your privacy. What I did was rude and aggressive and humiliating to you and your partner. My actions also affected your relationship with Dre, and that's not okay. Because of what I did, I made our home feel like a bad place for you and Dre to be. You have every right to be angry and upset. I was wrong to do that, and it was a huge overreaction.

I am so sorry for violating your privacy, ignoring our agreement, interrupting your date, and ruining your time with a loved one. I'm sorry for the pain I caused you and Dre. I wish I had never done that. I really, really regret what I did and what I said. I should have handled my jealousy in a better way, instead of taking it out on you. I don't want to ever put you in that position again. I want you to feel safe and respected in our home and in our relationship. I also want Dre, your dates, and loved ones to feel safe and respected.

Oliver and Malcolm discuss what happened more deeply. Malcolm says he never wants something like this to happen again. Oliver and Malcolm agree that it's time to talk about making amends and future behavior.

Oliver: I know it's my responsibility to deal with my jealousy. In the future, when I feel jealous or upset, I am going to go take a walk or get out of the apartment and make sure to respect your privacy. I don't want to use my jealousy as an excuse to control you and your access to your loved ones. I think that for the next few weeks it's best if I go out with friends or plan my own sleepovers away from home while you have dates over. I could use the time away to recalibrate myself and give you extra privacy. I'd also understand if you wanted to lock your door in the future.

Yesterday, I also made an appointment with a peer support counselor to talk about why I got so upset that night. I'm going to work with my peer support counselor until I feel I'm ready to be back at home when you have dates over.

I also owe your Dre an apology. I want him to feel welcome and comfortable when he's with you, not as though he needs to avoid me or avoid sleeping over. If you think it's a good idea, then I'll call him later today to say I'm sorry and clear the air.

How does this sound? Is there anything I can do to make you feel better and more respected when it comes to privacy? If you need some more boundaries around dating, sex, and closed-door stuff, then I'm really open to listening to what you need.

Why it's good: Oliver listens to Malcolm. He acknowledges his actions and their impact without getting defensive or accusatory and without trying to excuse his behavior. He's located the root emotion of his behavior (jealousy) and how it led him to act. He apologizes, expressing remorse and empathy for the hurt he's caused, not just to Malcolm but also to Dre. Oliver has thought about his plan for his future behavior. He is getting the support he needs via peer counseling, which will address his root emotion of jealousy. He's also removing himself from a potentially activating situation (being at home when Malcolm has sleepovers or dates) until he can handle these situations with more grace, patience, and compassion. He also plans to apologize to Dre, expressing his remorse.

Some things to keep in mind:

- After an error has occurred, you or your partner may need new boundaries, and that's okay.

- Sometimes even the most genuine apologies aren't enough. Respect the injured party's decision to forgive or not.

- Amends work only if you follow through on your plan.

- It may take a few conversations to move past an error.

- Accountability isn't always linear. Sometimes you may need to apologize and update your plan for amends more than once.

- A great strategy for any post-accountability conversation is writing a letter to the injured party, restating your acknowledgment, apology, and amends. A letter can be reassuring to the injured party and a follow-up commitment on the part of the person who needs to set things right.

- Being accountable builds trust. It feels *good* to apologize, treat your partners well, and make good on your promises.

Writing Your Own Apology Letter

Is there someone to whom you owe an apology? Write them a letter now, using everything you've just learned about accountability.

Situation

Acknowledgment

Apology

Amends

In the next section, we'll talk about community: how to find it, what it looks like, and how to handle the hard parts of community too. We'll talk about vetting, breakups, and how to find the balance between privacy, support, and safety. Then I'll give my final thoughts and a recommended reading list to keep you going and growing after you've finished this book.

SECTION 3

FINDING AND MAINTAINING COMMUNITY

Now that you've read about both the basics of polyamory *and* the tools to build and maintain a polyamorous lifestyle, it's time to talk about community.

Community is the lifeblood of *all* relationships because community is relational. You relate to your community; your community relates back to you. This give-and-take shapes who you are, your values, and how you move in the world. Your community is your family, your loved ones, your neighborhood, and your culture. It's the "everyone, everything, and everywhere" that you're connected to. It helps define and connect the dots of who you are.

In Section 3, we're talking about community: what it is and how to get it. Polyam community is extremely diverse, occasionally clandestine, and sometimes a little cliquey. So we're taking this in four main sections.

In Chapter 8, I'm doing something a little different with the Q&A. Rather than bringing in an expert for a discussion, I've asked my own polycule to join in a conversation about community. I don't believe there are any experts in polyamory. Of course, there are those with more experience, but I'm always a little critical of be-all and end-all expertise. I bring in my own loved ones, with the intention of allowing you a glimpse into the dynamics of a real, living polycule and to show that you don't have to be an expert, a sex coach, an author, a podcaster, or a counselor to be happy, secure, and successful in your relationships.

You'll hear from my fiancée, Salomé, whom I've mentioned throughout this book; Rachel, my partner and best friend, with whom I am long distance; my dear friend and former girlfriend Vanessa; and finally, Lorraine, my friend of many years, my recent lover, and someone very new to nonmonogamy. Their presence in my life and in this book is a blessing and privilege. Out of respect for my loved ones' privacy, I am not including last names or any identifying details.

In Chapter 9, I talk about what polyam community can look like and how you can find it. We go over a few strategies for meeting people who are nonmonogamous, with an emphasis not on *dating* or *sleeping with* the people in your potential community, but rather making meaningful connections that can be friendly, platonic, and familial. Remember: being non-monog isn't just about dating and sex. Sex is more a great side effect of the real pleasure:

your relationships and community. Nonmonogamy itself is about creating networks of care and mutual support.

Then, in Chapter 10, I talk about vetting—the safety practice of making sure someone is actually who they say they are—and what you'll need to know about interacting with others in community.

In Chapter 11, I talk about a messier aspect of community: breakups. I discuss how a polyam breakup differs from a monogamous breakup and how to handle one with grace and compassion, be it your own breakup or one in your polycule or community.

But we don't end on a sour note. I conclude with some final thoughts and well-wishes. My hope is that by the time you finish this chapter—and book—you'll know yourself better. The better you know yourself, the less bullshit you'll cause and deal with. And that's *always* a reason for celebration.

Chapter 8

IN CONVERSATION WITH A REAL-LIFE POLYCULE

I spent some time interviewing my own loved ones about community, queerness, and nonmonogamy. Because of scheduling, these interviews were done asynchronously, but it should be noted that my loved ones have their own connections and relationships with each other. Salomé, Rachel, and Lorraine are all friends and spend time together; Rachel and Lorraine live in the same city and went on a couple of dates; and Vanessa and Salomé dated for a year and a half. There are overlaps in relationships, and one of the great joys of community is seeing people you love form their own friendships and connections with one another.

I speak to Rachel, Vanessa, Salomé, and Lorraine. Pay attention to the ways they talk about finding and maintaining community.

SYG: Hi, can you introduce yourself? How long have you been nonmonogamous and can you briefly describe how we know each other?

Lorraine: Hi, I'm Lorraine. My pronouns are they/them. I started exploring polyamory and nonmonogamy around 2017. I know you—Sara—from school. We went to college together, and the first years we knew each other we were all fun-times friends, so we hung out at parties and at get-togethers. But with the years we connected a lot more and spent time getting to know each other. We definitely had crushes on each other back then too. *(laughs)*

Rachel: Hi! I'm Rachel, a writer and organizer in Miami, Florida. I'm queer and nonbinary, and use they/them pronouns only. I've been polyamorous since about 2016, so around six years. Wow, that feels like a lot to me. We know each other from Tinder, actually! We went on a double date with our partners at the time and hit it off. Since then, we've been platonic-ish partners and built a really beautiful relationship!

Salomé: Hello, I am Salomé (she/they/he). I have known I was theoretically polyamorous since I was sentient, and I've been practicing for about ten years. And I know you 'cause we're married. *(laughs)*

Vanessa: I'm Vanessa and I'm twenty-nine years old. I'm a first-generation Cuban American living in Florida, and my pronouns are she/they. I've been consciously polyam for nine years, but I've realized that it was possible and practical to love more than one person at once since my freshman year in high school. I hated myself because I caught feelings for two people at the same time. I remember sobbing and asking myself why I couldn't love more than one person. I felt so alone and ashamed. I've come a long way since then. I've been lucky to know you for two years. We met on Lex during Covid-19 lockdown, and our connection developed into a long-distance relationship that eventually included one of your partners. We're not romantically involved anymore, but we've remained friends.

SYG: How do you find and make community as a polyam person? Where do you go? How do you meet people? Do you organize events?

Rachel: This is a really good question. I think because I seek out specifically queer spaces, I interact with a lot of polyam people without seeking them out. I go to a lot of queer events like a queer Shabbat hosted by a friend and queer poetry readings. I think making an intentional decision like only wanting to be around queer people sets me up to meet people with a lot of the same interests and ideals (which is definitely not to say that all queer people are the same). I don't organize events necessarily, but I would be into it!

Salomé: The internet has definitely been a life-saving tool, especially when I was single and physically disabled. I am a very nomadic person, so it's been hard throughout my life to rely on physical communities. I would say I have a very strong virtual network. I've used this to help me find events or local people to connect with wherever I am in the world. In the past I have organized queer get-togethers. They weren't specifically polyamorous, but the type of people they tended to attract were queer polyamorous folks. I am a big fan of throwing well-hosted parties (you're invited).

Now, I also rely on my current relationships to expand my polyamorous community. Currently, my polyamorous community mostly consists of my partners' metamours, and that's how I build up my polycule. I don't rely as heavily on virtual spaces as I used to when I was younger, but it's definitely a tool I keep in my back pocket.

Vanessa: While I'm an extrovert, I don't specifically seek out polyamorous community in my day-to-day life. Online, I'm a part of a few locally based polyam social media groups, but I'm not very engaged or active in them. It's just nice to know they exist. Most of my community-building happens off-screen. I'm out as polyam in most social, family, and professional situations, so sometimes another polyam individual will hear me talking about my partners and find they can relate to my relationship structure, which I love! Meeting other polyam people in the wild is so delightful. It doesn't feel like having to come out for the billionth time. There's a shared understanding, which makes me feel more understood and safe.

I organize queer-centric events, and my partners come to most of my events. And sometimes they'll bring dates/partners or just other polyam people they know. Then those polyam people will come to the next event and bring other polyam people they know, and those polyam people bring more polyam people to the next event, and so on. It's exponential. They all mingle, make plans outside of the event, and bam, we've got a little community. It's so cool watching it form.

SYG: What is vetting in polyam communities?

Lorraine: I'm still tryna figure out what it looks like for me, but it's the process of getting to know a person/person(s) and figuring out compatibility in values, wants, needs, life plans, level of commitment, expectations, type of relationship one is looking for—really getting to know the person before deciding what type of relationship the parties involved desire and seek from each other.

The vetting process does not have a specific time frame to it, nor does it guarantee a formal relationship/partnership with someone.

Rachel: From my understanding of vetting, I think a lot of it gets done by word-of-mouth communication. Like, "I know this person has a past where they did this," or, "I thought this person was previously in a monogamous relationship." It's not quite gossiping, but I think it's important to know about people you're in community with. It's a lot of relationship-building. It's basically like getting to know who you're in community with and seeing if you're compatible and have similar polyam styles.

Salomé: My favorite way to vet people is when they're already established in a polyamorous network, and I hear good things from their community. However, I also know that people are constantly coming into polyamory and may not have the history to have references available. I think people who are new to polyamory are just as entitled to its benefits as those who are established. In those cases I like to ask them what polyamory means to them, what relevant experiences have they had, and what are their expectations for the realities of their current situation. I watch what they do versus what they say and how they treat the people I care about. I find it pretty easy to gauge if that person and I would be a good fit, based on their responses and general vibe.

Vanessa: All right, so I had to ask you to clarify what you meant by *vetting* in a polyam community, because I've only ever known the term to be used in the context of play parties or BDSM. Vetting in polyam communities has a similar goal of vetting in play parties and BDSM: they are questions about the other person's safe sex practices, experience with polyamory, and basically anything that has to do with the safety and comfort of the polycule.

SYG: Do you go through any vetting protocols when you meet a new polyam person you're interested in? What does that look like? Have you ever been vetted yourself? What was that like?

Lorraine: I think I just recently started implementing a more intentional vetting process with myself and the people I am interested in and also close friends too. I was under the impression that feeling intensely toward someone was the only signifier of attraction—liking or loving someone—and this has changed dramatically in the last few years. Vetting for me is based on asking and answering questions about who we are and our boundaries, going out on dates in a variety of contexts, engaging in activities the other person likes, and vice versa. Also engaging in conversations about our values, life theories, race, gender, religion, immigration, substance use, family relations, expectations around marriage, mental health, and general philosophies.

For me, vetting gets at the questions of, Do you actually like the person they are? And are you compatible, not just in personality, but emotionally, intellectually, spiritually, and geographically? I am new to vetting when it comes to emotional support. I am very guarded in that sense and feel like I am still developing what it looks like to show vulnerability to people and allow them to show me support. Being vetted is interesting because in the moment you realize you both are doing it, and it feels more human and it takes pressure from performing in ways that are just to impress.

Rachel: Honestly, vetting is a little too formal for me. I typically just have conversations with a person I'm into. Mostly, if I'm interested in someone and they are monogamous, I don't pursue anything even if they say that they're fine with polyamory. It tends not to go well, in my experience. If someone says they're open to polyam from the jump but has never been in a polyam relationship, I'm open to seeing what happens. Conversations I have tend to be around what cheating looks like for the other person, because I think it all depends on the arrangement. I also talk about hierarchy and primary partnerships, because those are things I don't align with. I've never been formally vetted, I think, but I have had really beautiful and intense conversations about what a relationship would look like and relationship styles.

Salomé: There are a couple questions I like answered before I choose how much to invest in someone. How often do you get STI testing? What's your practice on fluid swapping? And how much do you communicate with your sexual partners about these matters? This last one is pretty important to me, because if I get an STI it doesn't just affect me but anyone I am fluid swapping with.

I personally really enjoy Kitchen Table Polyamory, which is the idea that my partners and their partners could all be able to sit at a kitchen table without killing one another, ideally enjoying a shared meal. So when I meet someone new, I definitely want to know what their feelings are on metamours interacting. If the person and I have good vibes, but they don't want to do "kitchen table," I would still give them a chance, but it's something I consider.

And finally, I like to gauge how well they know their expectations and reality. My time and energy are precious. My partners' time and energy are precious. When you're trying to manage your schedule around multiple people, it's absolutely paramount that you know your limits and needs. For me to be able to invest in someone, I need to know exactly what their expectations are so I can realistically tell them if I can provide it.

I have been vetted by other people, and for me that looked like sitting down and talking it out: listening to them and their needs, and answering to the best of my ability the questions they had. Sometimes we'd find out we all got along great and we're ready to be best friends. Other times we found out it wasn't going to work out. But what was always critical was honesty, so that everyone involved could judge if this was something they could do.

Vanessa: I didn't realize it until we talked about it together, but I do conduct informal vetting when I meet a polyam person that I'm interested in. I don't structure it in a way where I'm asking them questions out of context, but I typically proactively offer my experiences and practices around things like safe sex, outness, and behavior specifically related to Covid-19, in the natural flow of conversation—or so it seems like the natural flow of conversation to me. I do talk a lot. *(laughs)*

These things are vital to have open communication about, and if they seem shy or reluctant to tell me what those subjects look like for them, then I'll circle back and specifically ask about it. At this point, everyone who I've been interested in would have given me an answer. However, if I was in a situation where I couldn't get an answer about, for example, what their safe sex practices are, we wouldn't have sex until a more in-depth conversation took place. I refuse to compromise my safety, the safety of my polycule, or the safety of our communities.

You and I mutually vetted each other online about Covid safety before we met. I know I felt a little nervous to share my needs because it wasn't like asking about safe sex, which isn't a hugely polarizing subject among queers nowadays. At the time, asking about Covid was politically, socially, and morally polarizing, with dangerous known and unknown health risks.

SYG: What's something you want everyone to know about finding polyam community? What are your words of caution? Your words of wisdom?

Rachel: My two guiding mottoes are "Trust your gut" and "Take your time." I think following your intuition is the best thing you can do for yourself, especially when getting into relationships. So yeah, I would caution people against ignoring red flags or little warning signs from your tummy. And what I mean by "Take your time" is that it's gonna take a good amount of time for you to figure out your preferred relationship style, communication style, and what kind of relationships really work best for you. Sometimes what you think you want turns out to be not true! It's trial and error, basically. It's hard and it hurts, but eventually it'll happen. Be open to new people and new experiences, but balance getting to know yourself and being in tune with your needs.

Salomé: I would say, remember that a community consists of individuals and each of those individuals are living their own unique reality. So when you're first interacting with a new space or place, don't write it off because of one bad egg, and vice versa, don't let one golden encounter tint your vision rose. A group will always have its angels and devils. And one person's angel may be another's devil.

Trust your gut. You will know when something feels right. And as you experience what feels good, you will hone that instinct. However, unnecessary judgment and critique of others will get you nowhere. If you want to shit on something just because it wasn't your cup of tea, you're going to have a hard time thriving in a practice that requires open-mindedness and finding ways to relate to a variety of people. Learn to know when you're reacting from your ego. Learn to know when to let shit slide. And learn to know when an issue needs to be discussed.

You're going to have to be brave. If this is the lifestyle you truly want, you aren't going to obtain it staying stuck in your old, unsuccessful ways. You're going to need to push yourself out of your comfort zone, you're going to have to work on yourself, you're going to have to own up to your bullshit, you're going to have to try things you never have and not let the fear of failure creep into your happiness. You're going to have to know how to love yourself and others.

Vanessa: Make sure that in any polyam community, whether it is in person or online, the space feels safe enough to advocate your own needs and that you aren't feeling invalidated. If you do see that happening, I think it's worth saying something about it! There is no obligation, but people need to be called out on their shit.

SYG: Especially when in community, a breakup doesn't just affect one or two people; it can affect an entire polycule and network of friends and lovers. What are breakups like when you're polyam? What have you learned about navigating breakups?

Lorraine: Breakups are hard and I feel like the concept itself is so intense, the way society has constructed it. There is so much pain involved in the process, and the idea of completely removing a person from your life from night to day can be overwhelming to our bodies and to our lives overall, especially in a community, where multiple relationships are being balanced. Something that I've experienced in the past is having insecurity in my support group after breakups because of the closeness in friendships with an ex-partner. I've closed myself off completely before to my friends because of that. I feel like boundaries were never established from me or my friends, which felt difficult to navigate, so I just chose not to "deal" with it.

Now I see the importance of being supported through such a painful process and the importance of communicating to others this anxiety and talking about boundaries that could both meet my need to feel supported and my friends' needs to balance being friends with an ex-partner. The main thing I've learned about breakups is the delivery and [thinking about] what the process of no longer being together is going to look like. I agree that there are times where having no contact with an ex-partner is necessary. If that is not the case, I want to practice having a gradual transition toward healing and friendship if that is desired.

Rachel: I think the answer is multifaceted. In my experience, polyam breakups include taking a lot of space despite it feeling like you'll see that person everywhere because you're in the same community. It's not that different from being queer: same friends, same circles, etc. It's a lot of creating boundaries for yourself about spaces you want to be in (or not be in) and how to care for yourself and your needs. Alternatively, it also means that you have a lot of support while going through a breakup. I think when you are intentionally making relationships that are all about expansive growth and connection, breakups can always be the same way.

Salomé: I think, being raised in a heteronormative society, our first indoctrinations into breakups is that they're sort of a spectator sport where you're expected to choose sides and swear the other party off as a sworn enemy until death. A lot of us had to bear witness to nasty divorces as kids, and that can really imprint on us. We had to endure ... navigating the clique networks of teenage creation, knowing our friends would dump us if we chose the wrong side during breakups. But I do fully believe that peaceful separation is possible and natural.

When you bring a new person into a polycule, you are asking your metamours to invest in that person. And hopefully they will, because that's how we build community. So if you end up breaking up with that person because of some incompatibility, you can't also expect your other partners to split with them too. That's a person they've taken time to form a relationship with that is absolutely unique and distinguished outside of whatever relationship y'all had. So if you're the kind of person who doesn't like to have exes in your life, then that's going to be a really serious chat you're going to need to have with your polycule.

I see it as a real invasion of privacy when I am asked to cut ties with someone. Obviously, I am not going to continue a relationship with someone who, without a doubt, has shown themselves to be a serial abuser with no intent to change. But if you expect me to take sides over some dispute riddled with a bunch of vague accusations and petty power grabs, then I will absolutely not engage.

Vanessa: Breakups suck in any relationship and relationship style. The hurt, grief, and loneliness that you feel isn't exclusive to just polyam or romantic connections. Almost everyone knows how it feels for a relationship to end. However, with polyam relationships, it can end up like a ripple effect. If you get dumped, it's going to emotionally affect you, which would likely affect your other relationships. Or let's say your partner is going through a breakup from a relationship where you had felt a lot of compersion, you might end up sharing some of that grief while supporting them through the breakup, which could put you in a similar emotional headspace and open you both up for better processing and dialogue. Some partnerships are more compartmentalized. You just have to trust and love each other and each other's emotions, and ask what ways you can support your partners during heartbreak. I've learned to ask for what I need and to lean on my community for support during breakups.

SYG: What's the best part of being polyam?

Lorraine: I think the best part of being polyamorous/nonmonogamous is how much room you have to explore and get to know oneself. People bring out different parts of you, and I think that's so beautiful and special and human. I think that witnessing that in other people is also very beautiful and so rewarding.

Rachel: Friends! Community! Being polyam has brought me some of my closest and most special relationships and friendships. It also challenges me in ways that help my growth in all ways. I learn about myself, and also I learn about a different way the world can be. It's helped my politics as well, and I see polyamory as being explicitly anti-capitalist. So yeah, basically I think the best part of being polyam is the expansiveness. Also, it's fun!

Salomé: I guess what I enjoy about polyamory is that I find it to be a system that tries to flow with human nature, instead of against it. I don't know of too many monogamous relationships where cheating hasn't occurred. And in my opinion that's pretty normal. Humans are social creatures. We have an innate desire to form relationships and explore with other people. Polyamory is as old as love. I don't really understand why we try so hard to fight that, and see it as such a breach of trust and moral failure when we cannot stay faithful. My take on it is if people are going to cheat regardless, why not just be open about it?

And it's not just cheating. In American society we are expected to oppress so many aspects of ourselves. We are expected to be strictly hetero and deny the variety of people we may be attracted to. We are expected to stick to our assigned gender at birth, even though we may fluctuate all over the gender spectrum throughout our lives. It's kind of exhausting to constantly fight my nature and something I am trying to intentionally do less of as I age. I just find myself so much more at ease when I am in community with people who understand just how dynamic humanity is.

My other favorite part about polyamory is the community. I love my partners and trust their judgment, so usually the people they love too are people I am just going to naturally vibe with. I love hanging out with a group of people that know love isn't a limited resource and that being a human is a lot more complicated than the textbooks taught us. It's constantly an uplifting space, where people know how to share their bounties and guide others to it without getting mired in their own insecurities or jealousy. I constantly find myself surrounded by people that want good for me, let me express myself as I am, and that just feels great.

Vanessa: I love being able to have relationships whose timelines and expectations aren't predetermined by a society who wanted to exclude queers, women, and other marginalized people. The freedom to explore satisfaction and community building in different parts of your life. Love, friendship (let's say you become friends with your metamour and remain as such after you and the initial relationship end). The pleasure that comes when you find it, and the curiosity, care, and expansiveness of it all.

SYG: What does dating mean to you? What is it like to have relationships with multiple people at one time? What have you learned?

Rachel: Great question! *Dating* is a word that people can have lots of different definitions for, as well as the word *relationship*. So for me, *dating* means making intentional time to build romantic or sexual connection without the same expectations that the word *partner* has. Dating multiple people at one time can be tricky and stressful. It's a lot of time management and honesty. I think you have to be as honest as you can. Always be explicit about what's going on. I've learned that saying something like, "I'm going on dates with this person and this other person too," to a date and allowing them to make up their mind about how they want to move forward is really helpful. But yeah, being honest and having open communication is really key because jealousy and time conflicts are definitely going to happen. It's just about managing them.

Salomé: I have no fucking idea what *dating* means. I am thinking about the endless memes on how lesbians will go on like sixty-nine "dates" with their best friend, wholly unaware that that's what they're doing. And honestly I feel that for multiple reasons. The primary reason being, as someone who believes in relationship anarchy, I think labels can really bog stuff down. It can create hierarchies and be leveraged in power dynamics. If I am investing in you, meaning I am spending time and energy on you, then I probably consider us to be some iteration of dating. In practice, if a person I am vibing with needs a label from me, then I will gladly sit down and discuss something that works for us, but I am also equally happy saying, "Listen, I like hanging out with you, and you like hanging out with me. And if that's good enough for you, then that's good enough for me."

I don't think having multiple relationships while polyamorous is that different than having multiple relationships while monogamous. Sure, we may use different language and have modified intentions, but at the end of the day what human doesn't have multiple important relationships. There's a lot of parallels. For example, I think a woman struggling with her jealous mother-in-law, who can't let her precious baby boy go, probably has a lot in common with a person struggling with a possessive metamour. I think a person having trouble establishing boundaries with their draining workplace probably also has a lot in common with someone trying to set boundaries with their polycule. Humans are social creatures. We are constantly navigating social networks and juggling the needs of a variety of people in our lives.

SYG: Anything else you want to say that I missed?

Salomé: Polyamory isn't complicated but being a human is. Don't conflate the two.

Chapter 9

COMMUNITY

Community is central to our happiness as humans. It provides us with a sense of belonging, connectedness, and purpose. Community reminds us we are not alone but part of something bigger.

In polyamory, a common misrepresentation is that it's all about sex. Sure, sex is an important part of the polyam experience. We are social *and* sexual creatures, after all. But polyamory, and nonmonogamy in general, is about much more than sex. It's also about community building.

Polyamory is a way to build a network of care, support, mutual investment, and aid. Community looks like the people you live with, your chosen family and sometimes your family of origin, the friends you can count on, the people you call when you need help or a favor, and the ones who call and lean on you. Community can also be the folks you connect with online, your long-distance loved ones, and people you bond with but never meet in real life. Community is whatever you make it, but it is *reciprocal*. Consideration goes both ways in community. And although everyone's community has a different shape, each fits the same need: the sharing of love, resources, and energy.

It's important to have variety in your community as well. Your inner circle of loved ones, such as a best friend, partner, or sibling with whom you share your deepest feelings and vulnerabilities, your midrange folks you meet at parties or for a casual lunch to laugh with and have fun, and your extended network, such as acquaintances at yoga or work whom you chat with.

As in polyamory, you can't have all your needs met by a single person. It's unrealistic and limits both you and your loved ones. You need the variety of relationships in your community to feel and be well rounded.

Where to Find Community

Finding community—the people who light you up, give great advice, challenge you, and make you laugh—can take time. If you're looking for a polyam-specific community, then there are a few tools you might consider.

Word of Mouth

If you feel comfortable, then start asking around. *Are there any polyam meetups? I'm looking to make some nonmonog friends. Do you know anyone?* You might be surprised by how many people in your life already practice some form of nonmonogamy.

Apps

There aren't a ton of apps that cater specifically to nonmonogamous folks, but apps are a good place to start if you're looking for friends and new connections. Make it clear in your profile that you're nonmonogamous and that you're looking for community; many other nonmonog folks do the same.

You might start out with Feeld (an app particularly popular with nonmonog and kinky folks); Lex (a queer-only personals app); OKCupid (an online dating app that uses quizzes and personality tests to find matches); and of course Tinder.

It is a messy world on apps though. You'll find a lot of unicorn hunters and people who fetishize marginalized folks. Before you dive in, think about how comfortable you are openly acknowledging your nonmonogamous lifestyle. You may see coworkers, babysitters, or neighbors on apps—and they'll be able to see you too.

Social Groups

Finding social groups and clubs can be extremely helpful in finding your nonmonog community. Think about your genuine interests—foraging? fermentation? art? book groups? sports?—and join something local. These groups don't have to be specifically nonmonogamous, but as I mentioned, you'll be surprised by how many people disclose they are polyam once you get to know them. If you're not inspired by the groups in your area, then start your own!

What do you want from your community?

Once you make the commitment to develop your community and expand your social network, it's important to think about the connections you want to develop. Are you satisfied with your romantic life but missing friends? Are you seeking more intergenerational dialogue? Does your community feel too insular and uniform in their opinions and beliefs? Do you want to feel more intellectually challenged?

Think about the community you want and what you can offer your loved ones.

What does my community look like right now?

What does my ideal community look like?

What are my deal-breakers for whom I will and will not be in community with?

What do I want from my community?

What can I give my community?

Chapter 10

VETTING

Vetting is the practice of making sure others are who they say they are and are *safe*, *compatible* people to have in your life. Vetting happens all the time in many contexts: interviewing for a job, checking references for a new dog sitter, Googling someone, asking a mutual acquaintance for information.

Vetting in the professional world is common practice, but these ideas can—and should— be applied to dating, relationships, and sex as well. Vetting is standard practice in the BDSM world. Why? Because BDSM and kink can be very risky from a safety standpoint, both emotionally and physically. If you're looking for a new play partner, then you'll want to make sure that they are trustworthy, are risk aware, and will prioritize your mutual well-being.

The same can be said of polyamory: it is risky. Your standards for safety, intimacy, ethical behavior, and honesty must be high in any type of relationship, but *especially* when more than just two people are involved.

For example, if you don't properly vet a new partner, then you might have a wonderful time one-on-one for many weeks. But when you introduce your new partner to your polycule, you might find this person is aggressive and rude. Why? Because you never had a proper, thorough conversation about their experience and level of comfort around interacting with other lovers. You might discover, after the fact, that they don't play nicely with others and aren't interested at all in the kind of relationship you want.

Or, as an even worse example, you might find out that your polyam partner actually *isn't* polyam. They've simply been using you for a secret affair, and their spouse has no idea you've been seeing each other.

That's why vetting should happen *before* you get emotionally, romantically, or sexually involved with someone else. Vetting can have many strategies, but I'll focus on three main groupings: conversation, references, and community.

Conversation

When it comes to vetting, having a conversation about who someone is, what they are looking for, and what their values are is nonnegotiable. This conversation ideally happens in the preliminary stages of any relationship. For me, these conversations often happen on the first meeting.

The point of having a conversation is to find out important, relevant information that will help you decide if the other person seems genuine, forthright, and compatible with you.

But remember, you're not grilling someone to try to catch them in a lie. And you're also being vetted yourself. Keep in mind the difference between a vulnerable question and an invasive question. Invasiveness might sound like, Tell me the most traumatic thing that's happened to you. But a more respectful, vulnerable approach might be, How do you typically handle stress or grief?

If you're asking someone a difficult question that makes them feel vulnerable, then you should also be prepared to answer a difficult question that makes you feel vulnerable. It goes both ways.

Conversation Starters

A list of conversation starters follows. These are open-ended questions that will help you get to know a potential partner or lover. They will also help clarify what *you* want, are looking for, and can realistically provide.

- What got you interested in nonmonogamy?

- How long have you been nonmonogamous? What kind of nonmonogamy do you practice?

- Can you tell me about your other partners? How do you all interact?

- What are you looking for in a relationship?

- How much time do you have realistically to dedicate to your relationships?

- What's your favorite way to spend time with a loved one?

- What's something you wish you'd known about love or relationships ten years ago?

- Have you ever dated someone of my [race, gender, sexual orientation, religion, and so on] before? What was that experience like?

- Can you tell me about a time you violated someone's boundaries? How did you handle that?

- What is your relationship to substances like?

- What's something you're working on in your relationships?

- What's your communication style like?

- Have you ever been to therapy?

- How do you handle jealousy or discomfort in your relationships?

- Are you friends with any of your exes?

- When was the most recent time you apologized to someone you cared about?

- How do you handle stress?

- What's your policy on safer sex?

Why it matters: A vetting conversation is an opportunity to ask yourself what you need to know about someone else and what you need to know about yourself.

References

References are particularly important if you're in the BDSM and kink community, but we can take their cue and extend this to nonmonogamy as well.

If you're interested in a potential partner, then ask them if they have any personal references: past or current lovers who can vouch for their behavior and trustworthiness. When asking for references, it's also helpful if you have your own references to offer as well, so it's an exchange, rather than a one-sided demand.

If you don't have references because you are new to nonmonogamy or don't have an ex who's comfortable sharing this kind of information, then be up-front about it. And be prepared to receive a no from the other party. Some folks don't share references on a first date because they find it an invasion of privacy or they prefer to introduce you to their other partners in person.

Why it matters: A reference represents a mutual opportunity to establish who you are and your capacity to have consensual, loving, and healthy relationships. References are especially important if you're looking for a sex- or play-based relationship or if you're connecting online or via apps rather than through a mutual friend.

Community

Finally, if you want to vet someone, then look to your community. Ask friends and lovers if they know a potential partner and if they have a good reputation. Find people whose opinions and intuition you trust, rather than random people you don't know well. There can certainly be a gossip mill in *any* community, so seek information from those you trust and can rely on.

Why it matters: When you travel in nonmonogamous circles long enough, you'll find a lot of overlap between friends, lovers, and metas, meaning people know one another either firsthand or through their polycules. Rely on your community and network to gather some basic information.

Red Flags in Vetting

There are a few red flags that can come up when vetting someone new. What follows isn't an exhaustive list, and only you can decide what is and is not a deal-breaker. But this list will help you get started.

- The other party is defensive, evasive, or dismissive when it comes to a conversation about values and past experiences.

- The person displays an inability to reflect on personal growth or past mistakes (for example, they're always the victim, their exes were all "crazy," and they've never crossed a boundary or needed to be held accountable).

- This individual has burned through a lot of partners in a very short time.

- They exhibit overconfidence and a lack of realistic thinking about scheduling, time commitments, sex, and so on.

- The person engages in virtue signaling: their actions don't align with their professed values.

- You experience a bad gut reaction.

The Polyamory Workbook

VETTING ACTIVITY

Now that you've gone through the basics of vetting, it's time you thought about what you need to know about a potential partner. Consider the questions that follow, but don't rush to answer them. Think carefully about what you really need.

1. *What are my nonnegotiables for a new relationship? Are my nonnegotiables fair, realistic, and based in mutual agency?*

----

2. *Where am I willing to compromise in a new relationship?*

----

3. *What information should I disclose before entering into a new relationship? Why?*

----

4. *What information do I need disclosed before entering into a new relationship? Why?*

----

5. *Would I be willing to date myself? Why or why not?*

Chapter 11

BREAKUPS: THE HARD PART OF COMMUNITY

No matter how close-knit your community, conflict always arises and breakups happen. As Salomé mentioned in our conversation, peaceful breakups are possible. This doesn't mean pain, grief, and uncomfortable transitions are absent, or even that you must stay friends after a breakup. But it does mean you are able to communicate your needs, make the best decision for yourself, and prioritize privacy and respect.

But a polyam breakup can feel *very* different from a monogamous breakup, often because there is so much overlap and enmeshment in your mutual relationships. A partner may break up with you but continue to date your girlfriend. You may break up with your partner, but they are still married to your best friend. You may have a mutual breakup but still see each other at parties, at community events, and on nights out. It can feel like everyone you know is watching something intensely personal happen. A breakup can seem to be a spectator sport of emotions.

For this reason, a polyam community is often more insular than its monogamous counterparts: on a practical level, there are just *fewer* nonmonogamous people than there are monogamous, so you rub shoulders with the same people more often. As a result, the way you de-escalate or end relationships can have an impact on your wider community and support network.

Frequent Causes for Polyam Breakups

Breakups happen for all sorts of reasons: a change in values, a change in circumstances, or a change in desires and needs. The key word here is *change*. All relationships change because people and our circumstances are constantly in flux. When thinking about breakups, it's important to remember that they don't represent failures. You can appreciate and honor the time you've spent with someone while acknowledging your dynamic needs to change. Sadness, regret, gratitude, and relief can all coexist.

1. Polysaturation

Polysaturation is a term used to describe when someone is at their limit for polyamorous relationships. Some people can maintain a maximum of two relationships. For others, it can be four or five. It depends on the person, the kind of commitments the relationships require, and external circumstances.

But when someone reaches overpolysaturation, it means they have committed to too many relationships. When you're overpolysaturated, you may feel overwhelmed, stressed, exhausted, and overscheduled. You may forget important dates, overbook yourself, or double-book yourself by mistake. You may be maintaining your relationships but have zero time for yourself, your own rest, or your own passions.

When people get overpolysaturated, this usually results in a de-escalation of some or all relationships, in other words, a reduction of commitments. Or it might result in breakups.

2. Closing the relationship

Sometimes a partner may decide to close their relationship and transition to monogamy. This usually happens in hierarchical polyam dynamics or between spouses with an open marriage: the "primary" relationship is preserved, and the secondary or unmarried partnerships are ended.

This kind of breakup can certainly come as a shock, but it usually arises for a few different reasons. A couple are monogamous, experiment with nonmonogamy, decide it's not for them, and close the relationship. In some cases, a long-term couple may be going through a difficult time emotionally and decide to close the relationship until certain issues are addressed. At other times, a health issue may force the relationship to close. Or of course it's not a mutual decision, and one partner is pressuring the other to close the relationship via ultimatum or coercion.

Regardless of the reason, breakups due to relationship closures can happen. Usually, the best thing to do in this situation is to cut your losses and move on. You should never attempt to convince someone to stay or become polyamorous: the decision is entirely their own.

3. Differences in values or needs

Finally, the most common reason for a breakup is a difference in values or needs (and this can happen in any sort of relationship style!).

For example, you may meet someone and connect on a deep, exciting level. You go on a few dates and have some conversations about your needs and expectations. You're on the same page: you want a casual relationship that does not escalate in any traditional sense (you don't want a live-in partner, you don't want to share finances, and you don't want to get married).

But as time goes on, you fall more profoundly in love with your new partner. You slowly realize your desires for the relationship have changed. You also realize your values are shifting too, and you do want a live-in, long-term partnership that is not casual or low-key. You tell your partner you want a more serious relationship, with room to grow and deepen your commitment. You disclose that you're thinking about the possibility of living together down the line and want to be up-front about it.

Your partner appreciates your candor, but their desires for the relationship have not shifted and they don't want the same things as you. You then talk about these incompatibilities, and although your partner wants to continue seeing you, you decide to end your romantic commitment. Together, you agree to transition to platonic friendship.

Changes in wants, desires, values, and goals are okay and happen often. What you may want on day one may change a few years down the line. This kind of breakup, like all departures, is certainly not a failure but a successful acknowledgment of difference and an adaptation to change.

We've reviewed the most common kinds of breakups that can happen in polyam dynamics. But how do you deal with them—especially in community?

Tips for Dealing with a Breakup

When a breakup occurs, you can feel the impact ripple into other parts of your community. Mitigating this impact, prioritizing privacy, and seeking intentional support can go a long way in minimizing this impact. A few tips follow.

Know When a Breakup Needs to Happen—and Don't Spend Time in Regret

A breakup needs to happen when your partnership is no longer adding joy, support, or richness to your life or your partner's. This may look like consistent arguments about the same issues without resolution; a lack of accountability; an increase in controlling behavior on one or both sides; a lack of mutual interests or boredom; or falling out of love.

Often our bodies tell us something needs to change before our minds realize it. Are you feeling stressed, tense, or trapped in a relationship? Do you feel relieved when you're alone and short-tempered when you're together? Talk to a trusted friend or therapist about these feelings, and ask yourself these questions: *Why am I in this relationship? Would I be happier with or without it?*

Once you've made up your mind, let your partner know. Have a gentle but firm conversation, and once it has concluded, don't spend time in regret. Grieve the loss, enjoy a new sense of freedom, and allow your emotions to take shape. But beware the what-ifs that often come after a breakup, and give yourself time to recalibrate before jumping into new relationships or trying to reignite old ones.

Decide What Needs to Remain Private

If you're going through a breakup, then chances are your polycule, community, and mutual friends will be informed one way or another. You should always let your polycule know what's going on firsthand, but think about what you want to remain private. Talk to your ex and see if there can be any agreements about what does and does not stay private. For example, you might have told your ex things that are not common knowledge to your wider community, such as heavy trauma you've experienced or rocky relationships with your family of origin. You might want this information to remain private, even after the breakup. Or you might simply want your breakup to stay out of the court of public opinion.

But you can control only your own actions and what information you choose to disclose or withhold. So choose wisely and with compassion.

Don't Gossip or Disparage Your Ex

Even though it can be extremely difficult—especially in the throes of emotion—to not disparage or gossip about your ex, restrain yourself.

There is a huge difference between venting or seeking genuine support and using gossip to take someone else down. You should certainly seek support from trusted loved ones, but gossip doesn't help anyone. Trying to set up your ex for difficulties in their community and friendships through half-truths and vague allusions to wrongdoing doesn't do anyone justice. It makes you look petty at best and your ex ugly at worst.

Of course, there is always context. If your ex was abusive and you inform your community and polycule of this fact, then you are disclosing important information—not gossiping or forcing anyone to choose sides.

If you find others trying to press you for details, then try a few simple phrases:

"I'm not going to get into it."

"I don't want to talk about that."

"My ex and I decided to end the relationship. I wish them well."

Don't Force Your Loved Ones to Choose Sides

Especially in polyamory, your loved ones and community will have their own unique relationships with your ex. It's unrealistic and unfair to request that anyone agree with you or stop associating with your ex just because you've broken up with them.

People make their own decisions about who their loved ones are. You can only work to protect yourself, make boundaries where needed, and disclose information as you see fit. Pressuring others to agree with you, dictating who they can and cannot see, or giving ultimatums undercuts another person's agency and freedom. Simply put, it is not your place.

Seek Genuine Support

The best thing you can do when it comes to a breakup is seek genuine support. Think about your support system. Who is a great listener? Who gives valuable perspective and advice? Who can distract you and have a great time? Do you need to see a therapist? Are you in need of a confidential peer support session?

Think about what you need and who in your community you can rely on. Think about the kind of privacy and level of support and advice you need. Then ask for help.

When a Relationship Needs to Change

When you're considering a breakup, a relationship de-escalation, or another big change, a great tool is a pros and cons chart. This chart isn't about marking the pros and cons of a *person*, but rather the pros and cons of what a change might look like. Framing matters here.

For example, a pro might be, "I'd have more free time to focus on myself and my passions if we break up," not, "My partner annoys me and gets in the way of my hobbies." A con might be, "I feel like I'm losing sight of what I want in my life," not, "It's my partner's fault I don't know who I am."

If you're not considering a breakup or de-escalation, then take this pros and cons activity to think about a past breakup and what led to it. You may notice some important patterns. Do you have a tendency to feel trapped in relationships? Do you have a tendency to smother your partners? Do you ever feel like you choose partners you know aren't compatible with you?

After filling out the chart, answer the reflection questions that follow.

Pros	Cons

What patterns did you notice while filling out the chart?

_____

_____

_____

_____

What does de-escalating a relationship look like? What does ending a relationship look like?

How do you know when it's time to de-escalate a relationship, create more boundaries in a relationship, or leave a relationship?

What kind of relationship do you want with an ex?

How can you tell when you and your partner are no longer healthy for one another?

Who can you talk to when considering changes to your life and relationships?

FINAL THOUGHTS

Polyamory, like life, is about love. It's about allowing love to inform your decisions, relationships, and self. It's about the freedom to love many and the freedom to love yourself.

You're now at the end of this book, and my wish is that you take what I've written as a sort of love letter, a gift of the love that I have in my life, the lessons I've learned from that love, and my love in sharing these parts of myself with you.

Love is grounding. Love is infinite. Love is the reason we make relationships, invest in their growth, find joy in connection, and mourn their loss. In moments of stress and doubt, I hope you can turn toward love and the resources I've shared here in their name.

Now let's take a minute to come full circle. At the start of this book, I asked you a few questions about control, freedom, and joy. I'm posing the same questions to you again—with a few additions. Take your time and think about what may have changed and what remains constant.

Taking a Final Moment

What is your personal definition of freedom?

....

....

....

What is your personal definition of control?

....

....

....

What does it look like for you to be in a relationship that prioritizes freedom?

....

....

....

What does it look like for you to be in a relationship that is controlling?

....

....

....

The Polyamory Workbook

Think of a time when you felt absolute joy and freedom. If you can't think of such a time, then invent it. Are you alone? With someone else? Describe how your body feels.

How have your answers, opinions, and desires changed throughout this book? Where have they not changed?

How do you make room for love in your life?

Why do you care about love?

How do you care for the love already in your life?

How do you feel about having a polyamorous lifestyle? What are your key values in nonmonogamy?

The Polyamory Workbook

RECOMMENDED READING AND RESOURCES

All About Love: New Visions **by bell hooks**

bell hooks was a Black feminist scholar, author, cultural writer—and one of the most important voices when it comes to love, capitalism, patriarchy, Blackness, and womanhood. In *All About Love*, hooks discusses love in a modern society and how we can reverse our cultural conditioning on gender roles, ego, control, and aggression to form new visions of love.

Bad Feminist: Essays **by Roxane Gay**

Bad Feminist is a collection of essays covering a range of topics like pop culture, food, race, domestic violence, empathy, social media, and more. When practicing polyamory, it's not enough to just read and learn about your relationships. You must also spend time reflecting on what informs relationships more generally, meaning your beliefs, cultural upbringing, and assumptions.

The Body Is Not an Apology: The Power of Radical Self-Love **by Sonya Renee Taylor**

Sonya Renee Taylor is a poet, activist, and educator. The book is an extension of Renne Taylor's work to "cultivating global radical self-love and bodily empowerment. [The movement] believes that discrimination, social inequality, and injustice are manifestations of our inability to make peace with the body, our own and others." The politics of your body, your community, and loved ones can't be ignored in an ethical polyam practice.

Come as You Are: The Surprising New Science That Will Transform Your Sex Life by Emily Nagoski

Emily Nagoski is a sex educator and researcher. In this book, she talks about sexual desire and how different people experience arousal. This is an excellent read if you're looking to better connect not only to your own sex life, but also to find new frameworks to describe and communicate your desires.

Communion: The Female Search for Love by bell hooks

Communion is the third book in hooks's trilogy on love. I recommend all three (*All About Love: New Visions; Salvation: Black People and Love; and Communion: The Female Search*). In *Communion*, hooks speaks to women specifically, but this should be read by folks of all genders to understand how love becomes an act of affirmation and freedom.

Damaged Like Me: Essays on Love, Harm, and Transformation by Kimberly Dark

Kimberly Dark is one of my favorite authors and this collection is especially wonderful, blending personal narrative with discussions of social hierarchy, body sovereignty, racial justice, and gender liberation. If you're looking to learn about these topics and how they show up in your life, add this book to your list.

The Ethical Slut: A Practical Guide to Polyamory, Open Relationships, and Other Freedoms in Sex and Love by Janet W. Hardy and Dossie Easton

This book is absolutely essential reading if you want more tools and resources in your polyam journey. It covers pleasure, intimacy, conflict, jealousy, and managing sexual encounters. Originally published in 1997, this book has had a massive impact on the language, ideas, and practice of nonmonogamy.

The Jealousy Workbook: Exercises and Insights for Managing Open Relationships by Kathy Labriola

I didn't cover jealousy extensively in this book—and for a reason. Jealousy is a symptom of controlling behavior, Big Feelings, and compulsory monogamy, so I paid attention to the root causes instead. If jealousy is an ongoing issue for you, I absolutely recommend you get this workbook as it's full of exercises, techniques, and proactive tips to not only manage jealousy in the moment but to prep you for times of crisis.

***Linked, A Polyamory Zine* by DaemonumX**

If you're not familiar with polyamory and BDSM coach DaemonumX, I highly recommend visiting their website. Their zine *Linked* is a great crash course in rules vs. boundaries, power dynamics, desirability, and privilege.

***Love's Not Color Blind: Race and Representation in Polyamorous and Other Alternative Communities* by Kevin Patterson**

People of color often experience discrimination, exclusion, and fetishization from white people in polyamorous community. Especially if you are white, you should read this book to understand how to identify and confront the racism in yourself and your communities.

***Pleasure Activism: The Politics of Feeling Good* by Adrienne Maree Brown**

Drawing from Black feminists like Audre Lorde, this book is a collection of essays, interviews, and poetry exploring sex, pleasure, gender, drugs, sex work, and so much more. I highly recommend this book to everyone interested in learning about why pleasure matters so deeply to people—and why pleasure is a main source of positive change in the world.

***Polyamorous: Living and Loving More* by Jenny Yuen**

Yuen is an award-winning reporter and her book not only offers practical advice for polyam people, but also the context and history to nonmonogamy and how perceptions around nonmonogamy are changing in modern times.

***Polysecure: Attachment, Trauma and Consensual Nonmonogamy* by Jessica Fern**

If you're interested in attachment theory and an in-depth look at how to forge secure polyam relationships with multiple partners, *Polysecure* is the place to start. This is a great book to read to help you understand all your relationships—familial, friendships, romantic, sexual, and so on—and how you tend to handle stress, conflict, and change in those relationships.

***Queer Ideas: The Kessler Lectures in Lesbian & Gay Studies* edited by CUNY Center for Lesbian and Gay Studies**

This book is on the more academic side of things, but if you're looking to learn from the absolute essential thinkers of gender, sexuality, class, race, and identity, this book has all the heavy hitters. *Queer Ideas* includes writings from Joan Nestle, Judith Butler, Eve Kosofsky Sedgwick, Esther Newton, Cherrie Moraga, Barbara Smith, and Monique Wittig. If you don't know these names, you will certainly recognize their contributions.

Queer Sex: A Trans and Non-binary Guide to Intimacy, Pleasure and Relationships by Juno Roche

If you are queer and/or trans, or have queer and trans partners, this book is wonderful, insightful, funny reading. Roche explores sex, pleasure, and dating with other trans and nonbinary folks. It's a great conversation starter if you want to talk about trans-centered sex and dating.

The Short Instructional Manifesto for Relationship Anarchy by Andie Nordgren

You can read Nordgren's manifesto, which I quoted in this book, for free at theanarchistlibrary.org. It's only a page, but distills the core ethics of relationship anarchy in accessible terms. I recommend printing it out and hanging it on your fridge.

Stepping Off the Relationship Escalator: Uncommon Love and Life by Amy Gahran

If you're looking to learn about creating and maintaining nontraditional relationships—the kind that don't have to end in marriage, mortgage, and children—this is a wonderful read. Gahran explores what the relationship escalator is and the various ways to opt out. I especially recommend this if you are looking to be in multiple relationships without predetermined social scripts or expectations

Ultimate Guide to Sex and Disability: For All of Us Who Live with Disabilities, Chronic Pain, and Illness by Miriam Kaufman, Cory Silverberg, and Fran Odette

Good sex is the kind that adapts to your body's changing needs, and the realities of your partners' bodies. I recommend you read this book if you are disabled, ill, or have chronic pain because it's a great source of support: there's illustrations, sex positions, sex toy information, and a robust resource guide with books and websites. Even if you are not disabled, read this book. You'll learn how to support potential partners and have a preexisting knowledge base to pull from.

Unfuck Your Boundaries: Build Better Relationships Through Consent, Communication, and Expressing Your Needs by Faith G. Harper

If you struggle to identify, create, and hold your boundaries, I recommend this book and its accompanying workbook. Harper identifies the different types of boundaries there are and how to use them in manageable, realistic ways. There's also great discussions on how to respect the boundaries of others.

Blackandpoly.org

Black and poly is a great resource for working definitions of different polyam terms, tips, and blog posts. If you are Black and polyamorous, you can also connect with other folks or attend meetups!

Polyamorouswhileasian.com

This site is run by Michelle Hy, a polyamorous educator and writer. Hy's mission is to destigmatize polyamory and make it more accessible and viable for everyone, but especially for BIPOC communities. Hy offers peer-support sessions and if you don't follow Hy on social media, I highly recommend it.

Shrimpteeth.com

Shrimp Teeth is run by Sam, who I interviewed in earlier chapters. The site has a wealth of resources on polyamory, and Sam offers peer-support sessions as well as workshops and activities. You should also follow *Shrimp Teeth* on social media for great infograpics and discussions.

ACKNOWLEDGMENTS

This book would not have been possible without a hearty support network of friends, lovers, family, and mentors. I am especially grateful to Sam and Crystal for lending their time and knowledge to this project. Thank you.

Thanks also to the lovers who have shaped me, held me, taught me. Thank you to the lovers who challenged me, showed me patience, and held me accountable. Thanks to those who have loved me well. Thank you to those who have not loved me well. These are lessons I won't forget.

Thank you to Rachel, my best friend and first reader, for your support, feedback, and encouragement. Thank you for how you see the world—and thank you for wanting to change it.

Thanks to Vanessa, who brings joy and community wherever she goes. Thank you for the love and generosity you've shown me. Knowing you makes me better.

Thanks to Lorraine, who offered up their thoughts and time to this project. Your intelligence, sensitivity, and laughter is a blessing on my head.

Thanks to Salomé, my partner in everything. I love you. This book would not have been possible without your wisdom, kindness, and generosity of spirit.

Finally, thank you to the whole team at Ulysses, but especially Renee Rutledge and Kierra Sondereker.

ABOUT THE AUTHOR

Sara Youngblood Gregory (she/they) is a lesbian writer. She covers sex, kink, BDSM, disability, pleasure, and wellness. Sara serves on the board of the lesbian literary and arts journal *Sinister Wisdom*. Her work has been featured in *TeenVogue*, *Vice*, *HuffPost*, *Bustle*, *DAME*, *The Rumpus*, *Jezebel*, and many others.

As a poet, Sara has been nominated for a Pushcart Prize, Best New Voices, and Best of the Net prize. You can find her work in places like Newfound Press, Cream City Review, and Ghost City Press. Her poetry chapbook *RUN.* is out now.

You may also know Sara as sinister.spinster from Instagram, where they talk about kink, polyamory, and sex ed.